Pakistan
Tradition and Change

Khawar Mumtaz and Yameema Mitha

Contents

First published by Oxfam (UK and Ireland), 1996
(0 85598 336 1)

Revised edition published by Oxfam GB, 2003
(0 85598 496 1)

© Oxfam GB 1996, 2003

Published by Oxfam GB, 274 Banbury Road, Oxford OX2 7DZ
www.oxfam.org.uk/publications

Printed by Information Press, Eynsham

Oxfam GB is registered as a charity (no. 202918) and is a member of Oxfam International.

LIZ CLAYTON

To the Masters of Cold Countries
(extracts)

... My country is torrid.
Maybe that is why one neither knows
of clouds which bring rainfall
nor of floods that destroy.
And to wreck my harvests, sometimes moneylenders,
sometimes wild beasts, sometimes calamities,
and sometimes self-styled masters arrive.

Don't teach me to hate my torrid country.
Let me dry my wet clothes in these courtyards
let me plant gold wheat in its fields
let me quench my thirst at its rivers
let me rest beneath the shade of its trees
let me wear its dust and wrap its distances around me.
...
The sun and you
can not walk side by side.
The sun has chosen *me* for company.

Kishwar Naheed,
translated by Rukhsana Ahmad.

Introduction

Located in the north-west of the South Asian sub-continent, Pakistan is a relatively new political entity. Comprising four provinces (North West Frontier Province, Sindh, Punjab and Baluchistan) and the tribal areas, northern areas, and the state of Azad Jammu and Kashmir, Pakistan represents a great diversity of topography, bio-climates, peoples, and cultures. The rural-urban division is sharp, as are the disparities between the rich and the poor.

The land was the home of ancient civilisations and the meeting point of great cultures: Buddhist, Greek, Muslim, and Hindu. Consequently, Pakistan has a rich heritage of architecture, folklore, art, and music. Its people share the common traits of hospitality, warmth, and friendliness, and a strong sense of dignity.

Born in the ferment of change that accompanied the collapse of colonialism, Pakistan is still a society in transition. Older forms of economic, social, and political organisation are under challenge, while new ones have yet to evolve. Trying simultaneously to meet the compulsions of the international market economy and the demands of its burgeoning population, Pakistan is searching for an appropriate system of governance, and struggling to define its identity. In the process it has experienced a wide range of conflicts resulting from economic disparity, authoritarianism, ethnic assertion, sectarianism, gender discrimination, external aggression, and Cold War rivalries.

This book attempts to capture the many facets of Pakistan: its beauty and richness, its scars and shortcomings, its people and environment – in order to understand better a society poised between tradition and change.

Village in Sindh province. Life in the villages of Pakistan has changed little over the centuries.

Busy street scene in Karachi, the largest city in Pakistan.

The land

Pakistan is bordered by Iran and Afghanistan on the west, China on the north, India on the east, and the Arabian sea on the south. It is separated from Tajikistan, one of the Central Asian Republics of the former Soviet Union, by a thin strip of Afghan territory in the north-west. The land is geographically diverse, including snow-capped mountains, plateaux, rivers, flood and arid plains, a variety of forests, deserts, lakes, swamps and a stretch of coastline.

Mountains cover more than half of the country's surface area, with three of the highest mountain ranges in the world: the Himalayas, Hindu Kush, and the

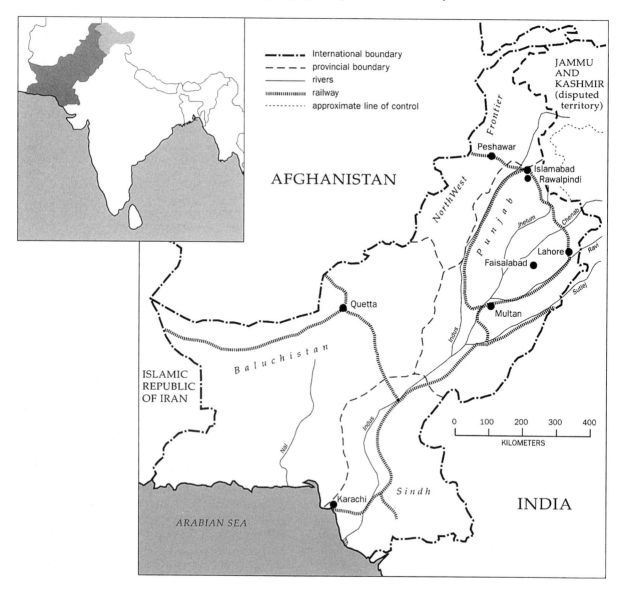

International boundary
provincial boundary
rivers
railway
approximate line of control

AFGHANISTAN

ISLAMIC REPUBLIC OF IRAN

JAMMU AND KASHMIR (disputed territory)

North West Frontier

Peshawar

Islamabad
Rawalpindi

Punjab

Jhelum

Chenab

Lahore

Ravi

Faisalabad

Sutlej

Multan

Quetta

Baluchistan

Indus

Indus

Nal

Sindh

Karachi

ARABIAN SEA

INDIA

0   100   200   300   400
KILOMETERS

Karakoram, which rise above 8000 metres. These formidable mountain barriers are broken by passes which have acted as gateways to invaders, armies, refugees, fugitives, and nomads, from time immemorial to the present day.

Climatic conditions throughout the country are very varied. While some parts of the regions get as little as 250mm of rain, others, such as north-east Punjab, receive as much as 1000mm when the monsoon winds blow from July to September. Temperatures are similarly wide-ranging, from -25°C at the highest elevations in winter, to over 50°C in parts of Sindh and Baluchistan during the summer months.

The other prominent physical feature is the 3200km long Indus River, traversing the entire length of the country, rising in the northern Hindu Kush and Himalayan mountains, and fed by five major tributaries. The river supports the country's complex irrigation system, the largest in the world, providing silt-enriched waters to the agricultural plains of Punjab and Sindh, before finally emptying out into the Arabian Sea.

The Indus

The Indus, cradle of ancient civilisations, has shaped the lives of the people living on its banks. The Indus valley cultures (2500BC to 1700BC) represent the first organised urban settlements in the world. Culture, art, and architecture flowered. Sophisticated irrigation systems and the first forms of writing were part of these early civilisations.

The Indus delta, covering some 3000 square miles, used to be extremely fertile. Thick mangrove forests fringed the coastline, there was a vast variety of marine life, and fishing communities

Darya Kabul, tributary of the Indus.

So the Indus delta died unwept, and with it a four-thousand-year history of trade and commerce... [as the water flow in the river declined] the sea moved into the lower reaches of the Indus distributaries for good, and the fertile mud flats became saline marshes unfit for cultivation. The rice mills ceased to function... large tracts of tamarisk forests died in the upper delta region. Drinking water was no longer available... it became impossible for animals or humans to survive... Those who could afford it, migrated along with their livestock.... Those who could not, moved away to work as landless labourers. The dhows unfolded their sails and sailed away from the Indus coastline...
(Arif Hassan, Herald, August 1989)

prospered. Much of the area has been affected by the construction of dams during the last 50 years designed to harness the waters of the Indus and its tributaries. Large tracts of desert lands became fertile, but at the same time the water flow to the sea was drastically reduced, changing the ecosystem and of the delta and destroying the livelihoods of the people that depended on it.

Deserts and plateaux

The Thar and Cholistan deserts in the Sindh and south of Punjab bordering India are marked by very low and erratic rainfall. But when the rains come, the deserts, particularly the Thar in Sindh, blossom into a veritable paradise.

There is a famous saying which is on every Thari's lips: 'Munjho muluk malir' ('My land is a paradise'). The phrase originated from a legend about Marvi, a beautiful woman from the Thar desert.

She was kidnapped and carried off by Prince Omar, and during her long years of captivity and exile, he would taunt her about her continual longing to return to her desert land, and she would always reply 'Munjho muluk malir'.

The Potwar Plateau in northern Punjab and the arid, sparsely populated Baluchistan Plateau to the south-west, also suffer from acute water shortages. Various indigenous methods were developed to store water. The most successful was a system of underground irrigation tunnels, *karez*, used in Baluchistan, which minimised water loss through evaporation. Tradition relates that some of the tunnels still in use were functioning when Alexander the Great arrived in this area. Many of the *karez* are now in a bad state of repair, but engineers are examining the system with a view to renewing it.

Valley near Gilgit, in the mountainous north-west of Pakistan. (opposite page) Carrying water, a precious commodity in the Thar desert.

NICK GARDNER

7

The four provinces

Pakistan now consists of four provinces: Punjab (63.9m people), Sindh (25.8m), Baluchistan (5.8m), and the North West Frontier Province (14.9m) In addition, there is the tribal belt (Federally Administered Tribal Areas, FATA), which for most purposes is treated as part of NWFP; and the disputed areas of Azad Kashmir and Gilgit Agency (total 3.5m).

Punjab is traditionally the most prosperous and dominant province. It is the main recruiting ground for the army and home for most of the big financiers and industrialists. Punjab is also the agricultural heartland of the country and pioneer of the green revolution. Most of Punjab's farms are owner operated, although there is a feudal belt in the south of the province where tenant farmers are in the majority.

The feudal structure in Sindh remains

(above) **In the old quarter of the city of Lahore, Punjab.** *(right)* **Wheat field in Sindh.**

much more intact than elsewhere in the country, with half of farms being run by tenants. The large landlords (*vaderas*) dominate their areas and can still command tributary labour. One consequence of feudalism is violence and insecurity, when *vaderas* give protection to robber bands (*dacoits*) that terrorise the area. Karachi, the largest conurbation in Pakistan, is in Sindh. It is now a city of about 9 million, and beset by all the problems of an overstretched urban infrastructure: pollution, overcrowding, poor services, ethnic violence, and crime.

Baluchistan is the largest yet most sparsely populated province, consisting predominantly of vast deserts and rough pastures. It is a largely tribal society, and the struggle between the Baloch and Pushtoon tribes for control periodically erupts into violence. The province is economically and socially under-developed. The arid conditions make sustainable agriculture difficult.

NWFP and FATA fall somewhere between Baluchistan and the rest of the country in terms of economic and social development, although their social structure is much closer to that of Baluchistan. The south of the province

includes a canal-irrigated zone, dominated by small farmers, not unlike northern Punjab. The rest of the province is mainly mountainous, with rangelands and rain-fed agriculture, or small-scale irrigation. NWFP is also a tribal society, and 68 per cent of the farms are owner operated. There is a shortage of employment and resources for the expanding population. Deforestation is a serious environmental problem.

Terracing showing up under the snow, on a steep mountain slope in North West Frontier Province.

Nomad encampment, Baluchistan.

The people: an ethnic mix

The riverine plains are home to the majority of Pakistan's people, the Punjabis and the Sindhis; the Pathan tribes live in the north-western mountainous region; and the smaller but distinct nationalities (the Kalash and the people of Chitral, Gilgit, and Hunza) live in the extreme north. The Baluch and some Pathans live on the Baluchistan Plateau, and the Seraiki-speaking people in the south of Punjab. The Punjabis, including the Seraiki speakers, constitute roughly 55 per cent of the population, Sindhis 20 per cent, Pathans 10 per cent, *muhajirs* (those who migrated from India at the time of independence in 1947) 7 per cent, and the Baluch about 5 per cent. There are also several sub-groups, such as the Brohis of Sindh and Baluchistan, the Seraiki speakers of Punjab, the Hindko speakers of the Frontier, and the Persian speaking Hazaras of Baluchistan, who consider themselves ethnically distinct. All these distinct peoples represent a wide variety of culture, language, dress, art, and literature.

Gypsies, in Sindh province. Many of them work as day labourers in the fields.

Family in a village in Punjab, making rush-mats for sale.

BEN BUXTON

(left) Woman from a community of brick-kiln workers.

DAVE TOMSON

LIZ CLAYTON

(above) The village midwife, in a village near Lahore, Punjab.

(left) Herdsmen in Quetta, Baluchistan.

A turbulent history

Pre-historic beginnings

Human history in Pakistan goes back to the stone age. Relics of the earliest stone-age man (500,000 to 100,000 years ago) have been found in northern Punjab. The Baluchistan Plateau culture, developing later (4000 BC to 2000 BC), extended to Iran. This was the precursor to the Indus valley civilisation (2,500 BC to 1700 BC), one of the earliest examples of organised urban settlement. This agrarian civilisation, the largest in the ancient world, stretched along the Indus river and its tributaries from the Himalayan foothills to the Arabian Sea. Excavations have revealed well-planned cities in Harappa (Punjab), Mohenjodaro (Sindh), and other sites in lower Sindh.

Since those first Dravidian settlers of the Indus Valley, successive waves of Aryan migrants from Central Asia came to this region. Alexander of Macedonia invaded with his armies in 327-326 BC, defeating local rulers on his journey from Gandhara, in the north of the region, to the south and west. Though Alexander stayed only for two years, the influence of Greek culture endured much longer. A Hindu dynasty, the Mauryans, succeeded Alexander (325 BC – 185 BC) and founded the first Hindu Empire. Ashoka, a later Mauryan king, adopted Buddhism, the new religion flowering in the Indian sub-continent, and Gandhara became the centre of Buddhism. Traces of a fusion of Greek, Central Asian, Indian, and indigenous cultures can still be seen in the ruins of Taxila city, in the Kalash valley, Gilgit, and Peshawar.

By the seventh century AD, Buddhism declined completely and Hinduism became the dominant religion. Around this time the Arabs, who had trade and commerce links going back for centuries, came for the first time as conquerors (712 AD). By 724 AD they had established direct rule in Sindh. Muslim rule, finally consolidated under the Mughals, continued over most of India until 1761. By this time, European trading companies, Portuguese, British, French, and Dutch, had become well-established in the sub-continent and were spreading their political influence.

(above)
Seal discovered in Mohenjodaro. The bull was a sacred animal in the religious rituals of the Indus valley civiliation. The inscriptions on the seal are one of the earliest forms of writing.

(right)
Mughal Empress, Noor Jehan, from a miniature painting.

Mohenjodaro 2500BC–1700BC

Mohenjodaro, situated on the bank of the Indus, is one of the world's most spectacular ancient cities. Well laid-out, with wide streets and spacious houses, and a complete drainage system, the city remains a monument to an advanced and complex civilisation. Most houses were two-storeys high, with fair-sized rooms arranged around an internal courtyard and bathroom. The latter had a circular well and drain that emptied into a cess-pit from which water entered the main covered drain in the street. The artefacts, jewellery, figurines and seals found on the site reflect a highly-developed and sophisticated culture.

Colonial encounter

The land that is now Pakistan has always been a passage through which outsiders came and conquered the rest of India. The fertile plains of Punjab in particular were attractive to successive groups of invaders. In the period between 1798 and 1818, the British had managed not only to oust their fellow-European competitors, but to transform themselves from traders to an imperial power that had established indirect rule over most of the region. British power was challenged by many Indians – landlords, petty rulers, and nominal princes – in an organised resistance in 1857. This is known as the 'War of Independence' in Indian and Pakistani versions of history, and 'The Indian Mutiny' in the British version. The resistance was crushed, India was declared a colony of Britain, and direct rule imposed.

The impact of the British on the Indian sub-continent has been very deep. They brought with them a world-view based on their experience of the industrial revolution. They introduced changes in social and economic structures, and in systems of production, which served British interests and were not always in harmony with local needs: the shift to cash crops like cotton to provide for the British textile industry; the resettlement of large numbers of people from other areas; and the breakdown of subsistence agricultural systems. Railways were built, for moving agricultural raw material and other goods for the British markets, which made people more mobile than ever before.

Such modernisation brought tremendous social changes in a very short period of time. The British introduced new systems of revenue collection, legal procedures, forms of education, civil services, and politics, which in turn affected social relationships. The powers of traditionally dominant groups were reduced, and a new class of professionals (doctors, lawyers, and teachers) emerged that modelled itself on the British.

During the political struggles that took place under British rule, new ideas of democracy, freedom, and nationalism developed, which were to provide models for the systems and institutions of governance after Independence that continue to be followed to this day.

Pakistan's cultural heritage

As an area with a turbulent history and the meeting place of many cultures, Pakistan's traditions are rich and varied. The constant influx of settlers, traders, and invaders from Persia, India, China, Turkey, Greece and Afghanistan, have all left their mark on the art, crafts, architecture, dance, music, and literature of Pakistan.

Language

Linguistically Pakistan is a heterogeneous country, although all the languages now share variants of the Arabic-Persian script and alphabet. Urdu is the official language, developed during the Mughal times to serve as a common language for their eclectic army. Because it was primarily the language of the educated Muslims of northern India at the time of Independence, Urdu became strongly associated with Muslim nationalism. English is used along with Urdu for official business and in some parts of the education system. In most of Pakistan, it is the language of the elite and upwardly mobile.

Urdu has become politicised over the years. Mother tongue to the migrants from northern India (*muhajirs*), it has become their symbol of identity. Despite some resentment against it, Urdu has developed, and remains the language of literature and poetry. Some of the most sophisticated as well as popular poetry is written in Urdu, and the majority of newspapers, magazines, and books are published in that language.

While Punjabi, the mother tongue of the majority of the population, is not read by many people, due to difficulties with the script, Sindhi, written in a variant of Arabic, is the most developed among the regional languages of the country. It is rich in both language and literature, although Sindhi culture in Pakistan suffered considerably at Independence, when most of the educated, middle-class Sindhis, who were Hindus, migrated to India. Since a large number of Urdu-speaking migrants from India settled in the cities of Sindh, the movement for the promotion of Sindhi language and culture has been expressed in opposition to Urdu. This has led to conflict, in 1972 when language riots occurred after the government decision to grant special status to Sindhi language in the province.

Pashto, the dominant language of the NWFP, has a rich oral tradition. In the province of Baluchistan the prominent languages are Balochi and Brahui. One of the main dialects of Balochi is called Makrani, from the city of Makran near the border of Iran. Brahui is the only Pakistani language of Dravidian origin.

(facing page)
Most people in Pakistan, men, women, and children, wears a variation of the *shalwar kameez* – loose trousers and long shirt. While fashion dictates colours and designs for every-day, each district has its own traditional distinctive shapes, colours and techniques, and patterns of embroidery and decoration. *Saris*, *dhotis* (a sort of sarong), and *lehengas*; *chooridars* (tight trousers which roll up like bangles when worn) *ghararas* and other elaborate skirts are also worn. Styles in women's *dupattas* – long scarves worn around the shoulders – vary too, with regional differences in size and thickness. Men's hats are also distinctive – from the rolled-felt hats of Chitral, to the colourful, embroidered caps of Sindh.

LIZ CLAYTON

DAVE TOMSON

DAVE TOMSON

RICHARD TALLONTIRE

ZEHRA HASSAN

15

A land of poetry

Every Pakistani is a poet. Man, woman or child, literate or illiterate, Brahui or Urdu speaking, nearly everyone has composed a few verses some time in their lives. A Pakistani poet may be an old Baluch out grazing her animals in the desolation of majestic mountains, a fisherman singing in the starry night in a boat far out at sea, a Pashtun with his gun slung over his shoulder, a brick-kiln worker at a union meeting, a young college girl serious and romantic, a clerk in a musty office, a rickshaw driver painting his verses on his vehicle, village women at a wedding party, a devotee at a saint's shrine, a Sindhi farmer at a *kutcheri* (talking together in the evening), a villager at a *tanzeem* meeting, or a poet at a *mushaira* (a poetry reading session where a candle is passed from person to person as they read their verse).

Some people may be too shy to recite their own poetry to you, but everyone will launch into verses by the well-known poets in the course of ordinary conversation. Poetry is set to music in the form of the *ghazal*, where the music is subservient to the words. In a *mushaira*, or a *ghazal* concert, the audience will applaud the verses they like best, and the poet or performer will repeat them. *Mushairas*, formal or informal, impromptu sessions with friends, are a favourite activity for Pakistanis.

There is a national festival to celebrate the birthday of the late Faiz Ahmad Faiz, Pakistan's greatest poet. After the death of a young woman poet, Parveen Shakir, in a car accident recently, a national day of mourning was declared.

Pakistani poets have been in the political forefront of the fight against oppression, and even those who do not agree with them politically will savour the flavour and quality of their poetry.

The tradition of the Sufi

Popular traditions continue, almost unaffected by political upheavals. Traditional poetry, literature, art, dance, music, crafts and architecture of Pakistan reflect the influence of Sufi thought. The Sufi's quest to 'know', to 'understand' is through creative expression. Sufi thinkers have contributed much to the country's poetic heritage, and their poetry, in particular, has developed its own symbolism over time. In Pakistan it represents resistance to authoritarianism and state oppression, and of freedom of the spirit and soul. This spirit of resistance continues in contemporary times in the work of poets like Faiz Ahmad Faiz and Habib Jalib. All the Sufi saints are remembered by their poetry.

'Reciting the names of God on your rosary, and looking pious
Will never make you into a good Muslim
For within your heart lie hidden,
Deceit and Satan.'

Shah Abdul Latif Bhitai, Sufi Sindhi poet

Dedication (extracts)

Let me write a song for this day!

This day and the anguish of this day
For this wilderness of yellowing leaves –
which is my homeland.
For this carnival of suffering – which is
my homeland.
Let me write of the little lives of office
workers
of the railmen
and the tonga-wallahs
and of the postmen.
Let me write of the poor innocents they
call: workers.

Lord of all the world
promised heir to all that is to come.
Let me write of the farmer
this Lord whose fief was a few animals –
stolen
who knows when;
this heir who once had a daughter –
carried off
who knows where;
this chief whose turban is a tattered rag
beneath the feet of the mighty.

... Let me write of the students
those seekers of the truth.
Who came seeking the truth at the
doorstep
of the great and the mighty.
These innocents who, with their dim
flickering lamps came seeking light
where they sell naught but the darkness
of long endless nights.

Let me write of the prisoner in whose
hearts all our yesterdays
dawned like sparkling gems.
And burning, burning through the dark
winds of prison nights
are now but distant stars.

Let me write of the Heralds of the
coming Dawn ...

Faiz Ahmad Faiz
(Translation by Shooaib Hashmi)

Faiz Ahmad Faiz, regarded as Pakistan's greatest poet.

Working woman (extracts)

They all say
I am too proud.
That I bloom and blossom with the
efforts of my own sweat and blood.
Every leaf is watered by the sweat of my
brow...
I am like a tall tree.
Yet within me there is an ancient creeper
which sometimes –
when the gales are strong –
wants to find a strong branch
round which to wrap itself.

Parveen Shakir

Music and dance: classical and folk traditions

Traditional dance and music takes two forms, classical and folk. While the classical expressions of both art forms developed under the patronage of the court or priesthood, the folk traditions are expressions of people's joy or celebration at particular times in their lives: the birth of a child, a marriage, a religious devotion, or a spiritual experience. In Pakistan, classical music and dancing have suffered neglect and deliberate discouragement under some governments, particularly that of General Zia. But committed teachers continued to teach and students to learn, in an environment that was extremely hostile. They persevered, and it was a revelation after the end of Zia's rule not only to rediscover the great teachers, but to see new young stars burst upon the horizon, performers of a quality that was second to none.

Ghazal, poetry sung to a musical accompaniment, is very popular, as is *qawwali*, a form of devotional group singing. Leading *qawwals* like the Sabri Brothers and Nusrat Fateh Ali Khan are not only extremely popular in Pakistan but have also popularised *qawwali* in the West.

(right) Tehreema, classical dancer.

(below left) Rubina is a professional folk dancer. She, her mother, and her sister, sing and dance for the women at weddings. During the wedding season they are scarcely ever at home, and can earn between 500 and 5000 rupees for each engagement.

(below right) Musicians playing for dancing at a festival.

Folk music, closer to the people, has not faced any constraints, and has continued to flourish. Folk instruments include many versions of the flute, percussion instruments, including the *matka*, an earthen water vessel, and the *chimta*, a long poker. The most commonly played instrument in Pakistan is the *dhol*,

a double-sided drum, which takes several forms. The *dholki* is a small drum played flat on the ground, usually by women, at any and every festive occasion from weddings to Basant. It is accompanied by singing and folk dancing. Wedding celebrations last three days or more, one day being given over to the *mehndi*, when the bride's hands and feet are dyed with an intricate clay pattern of dark red henna, and there is much singing and dancing. The *dhol* is a larger drum, hung round the neck and played with sticks, normally by a man. It is used outdoors, to dance to, or to accompany professional singers. The *tabla*, a twin drum set, is used mostly for classical accompaniment, and is one of the most complex musical instruments of the subcontinent, on which every note on a musical scale can be sounded.

Basant: the kite-flying festival

Basant: the sky is full of a thousand coloured kites,there are parties on the rooftops, blaring music and the hypnotic beat of the *dhol*, and gangs of little boys yelling 'Bo-kata!' and chasing something just beyond the horizon.

The kite-flying festival is celebrated with passion and abandon in the city of Lahore. It heralds the advent of spring after the cold winter and is a traditional festival of the Punjab, associated originally with farmers. During times when the state comes under religious influences, there are efforts to discourage what is, after all, not a religious festival. Lahoris have simply ignored such attempts with aplomb.

The colour of the day is yellow and everyone, especially the women, wears yellow. Yellow food is cooked, vegetables, specially cauliflower or potatoes with turmeric, yellow sweet rice (*zarda*, which means yellow), and Basant is a party day. People get together in open grounds or on roof tops to fly their kites. A great deal of care goes into preparing and stringing the kites before they actually fly.

The festival goes on all day, and when darkness falls, huge search-lights light up the sky, white kites are flown from the roof tops in all parts of the city, the rich homes of the elite as well as the congested homes of the walled city, once the heart of Lahore town, and the festival continues all night.

A feature of kite flying particular to Punjab is a competition to cut other people's string, and young boys chase after the fallen kites as booty. Kite flying around the time of Basant becomes an obsession. Kites sell for as little as 20 pence and as much as £25. But the real cost is the *dor*, the string. Connoisseurs will get their string prepared the summer before, spending hours lacing it with ground glass to ensure its cutting edge! All over the pavements of Lahore, shocking pink and royal purple string is stretched out to dry, laced, and stretched out again by sellers of *dor*. String for the day of Basant can cost anything from £5 for a large party of children to £200 for three or four adults.

Women take part in all the activities of Basant, but to actually cut another person's kite is considered somewhat tomboyish! The phrase used for one kite battling with another is *pecha larana*; and the same phrase is used for a flirtation.

Selling kites for Basant.

19

Young cricketers, Baluchistan.

Olympic champion in hockey, and the country has produced top-level squash players like Jahangir Khan and Jansher Khan, the current world champion.

Other favourite sports include *guli danda*, a street game which some consider to be the precursor of hockey, played with a stick and a four inch long elongated 'ball', *kabadi*, where two teams of players, with oiled bodies, try to slip across to each other's territory, wrestling, and *buz kushi*, an early form of polo played in the northern mountains.

Architectural expressions

Architecture in Pakistan displays great regional diversity, based on available building materials, environmental factors, and social requirements. Succeeding historical periods have had their own distinctive styles, and have influenced that of successive periods. The Buddhist Gandhara architecture, for instance, strongly influenced subsequent Hindu architecture of the Salt Range (650-1026 AD). This, in turn, was assimilated in part by the architecture of the first Muslim Kings, and can still be traced in later tombs in the cities of the south Punjab. The Mughals who followed in the sixteenth century left a rich heritage of buildings with their lavish construction of imperial forts, palaces and gardens. The Fort, Badshahi mosque, Emperor Jehangir's tomb, and the Shalimar Gardens in Lahore are fine examples.

The British colonists brought with them the building style of the contemporary West, still to be seen in buildings like the High Court and Chief's College, in Lahore, and Freire Hall, the Hindu Gymkhana and the Sindh Club in Karachi.

Sport

Sports play a major part in the lives of Pakistanis. Cricket has become a national passion and children can be seen playing the game in the streets or any open spaces available. When the national cricket team is playing a match, life in the country comes to a standstill. Public holidays are declared when the team wins an international game (which it often does). Cricketers like Imran Khan, Wasim Akram, Javed Miandad are superstars in Pakistan.

Field hockey and squash are also popular, though they do not have the glamour of cricket. Pakistan has been the

MARYAM IQBAL

(left) Shalimar Gardens, Lahore.

RICHARD TALLONTIRE

LIZ CLAYTON

(far left) Old mosque in Karachi.

(left) Doorway, the Fort, Lahore.

(below) Shrine at Multan, Punjab.

MARYAM IQBAL

The birth of Pakistan

An Indian nationalist movement opposed to the British emerged with the formation of the All India National Congress in 1885. Muslims supported the Congress initially, but with the increasing use of Hindu symbols and rhetoric by Congress, which contradicted its claims to be an all-India party, the Muslims became more and more alienated.

In 1906, the Muslims formed their own political party, the All India Muslim League. Initially, the League saw its role as safe-guarding and representing the interests of the Muslims of the sub-continent. Its early preoccupation was to ensure Muslim representation in the parliamentary institutions that would be set up in post-independence India. It was the Muslim poet-philosopher, Muhammad Iqbal, who first put forward the idea of Hindus and Muslims having separate national identities. This idea crystallised in the 1940s into a movement demanding a separate homeland for Muslims.

In 1947, the British finally left. Pakistan was born as an independent state in two parts: West and East Pakistan, separated by almost 1000 miles of Indian territory.

The controversial demarcation line between India and Pakistan was drawn hurriedly and almost arbitrarily. The process of Partition involved a massive upheaval of populations: some 14 million people crossed the new boundary: Pakistan lost six million people, mainly Hindus, and gained 8 million Muslim refugees from India. One million people died in the violence which accompanied Partition; thousands were displaced.

The influx of people from India added yet another element to an already complex racial-ethnic composition of the country. It sowed the seeds of conflict and discord for the years to come. Even now the migrants of 1947 are not fully integrated with the local population, particularly in Sindh.

Building a nation

West Pakistan, where the seat of government was located, had not existed as a political unit in undivided India. Sindh was part of the Bombay Presidency; Baluchistan and a substantial part of NWFP had resisted coming into the fold of the British administrative system and were largely governed by the

---

Jinnah's address to the Assembly: 11 August 1947

'...You may belong to any religion or caste or creed – that has nothing to do with the business of the state. We are starting in the days when there is no discrimination, no distinction between one caste or creed and another. We are starting with this fundamental principle that we are all citizens and equal citizens of one state...

Now, I think we should keep that in front of us as an ideal and you will find that in course of time Hindus would cease to be Hindus and Muslims would cease to be Muslims, not in the religious sense, because that is the personal faith of each individual, but in the political sense as citizens of the state...'

tribal codes of rival chiefs; Punjab was the most organised and developed province. Its major city, Lahore, had been the provincial capital and a leading centre of education. But it was Karachi, the tiny port city of Sindh, that was selected as the new capital.

Pakistan did not inherit well-established administrative, political, economic, and military structures. Most of the assets and state machinery went to India. The country had almost no industry, or mineral resources. The number of professionals was tiny. The civil and military bureaucracies, though fragmented and weak, were the only ones that functioned.

The Constituent Assembly, consisting of Muslim members elected to the Federal Assembly and the Council of States in the Indian elections of 1946, was the primary political institution. The new country faced many challenges: rehabilitation of refugees; reconstruction; economic development; setting up of administrative institutions; and infrastructural development. The most important task was to formulate a constitution that would embody Jinnah's vision of a non-theocratic, liberal, democratic Pakistan, where the freedom of speech and conscience of all citizens would be secure and tolerance, human dignity, and emancipation of women ensured.

The task of building a nation from scratch was indeed formidable but there was an equally vast opportunity to remodel and develop structures of governance and economic and social management according to the needs of the people. However, issues of ideology and politics, division of power, form of government, tensions with India, among others, kept consensus at bay, and meant that this opportunity was lost.

The disadvantages which the newly-born Pakistan inherited were compounded by a number of unforeseen occurrences: Jinnah's untimely death hardly a year after Independence; the first war fought with India over Kashmir (1948), instilling a permanent feeling of insecurity and threat; the assassination of the first Prime Minister, Liaquat Ali Khan. External factors have had a strong impact on internal developments. For example, the tense relationship with India (marred by three separate wars) has been central to Pakistan's foreign policy, and was one of the reasons for the military alliance with the US, and unfriendly posture towards the Eastern bloc countries. Events such as the Afghan war and the Iranian Revolution have had a profound effect on Pakistan's internal stability and foreign relations.

Power and politics

Pakistan has been ruled by military dictatorships for almost half its existence (1958-1972; 1977-1985). The country has seen frequent dissolution of elected assemblies, the banning of political parties and trade unions, the curbing of student activities, and press censorship. As a result, the development of political and social institutions has suffered. The economic consequences of dictatorship have been sharper inequalities between different sections of society, and between different regions, and great concentration of wealth in the hands of the few. During Ayub Khan's period, 66 per cent of the country's industrial capital was owned by 22 families.

The country experimented with various forms of elections on its bumpy political path. There were direct elections; indirect ones; 'basic democracy' elections whereby a limited electoral college was first voted for on universal adult franchise, which in turn elected the President; and non-party elections. The first general elections on the basis of universal adult franchise were held in 1970, 23 years after independence, under the military government of General Yahya Khan, and were acknowledged to have been free and fair. Stability proved elusive to civilian governments as the political leadership failed again and again to share power and agree on systems of governance.

Dates and Events

1885 First Indian National Congress meets in Bombay.

1906 Foundation of the Muslim League.

1920 – 1922 Gandhi's Non-Cooperation Campaign.

1928 Indian women granted voting rights equivalent to men.

1932 All India Muslim League supports women's demand for equal rights for all people regardless of religion, caste, creed or sex.

1940 'Two Nation' theory articulated by Jinnah.

1942 – 1943 Bengal famine.

1947 Independence and Partition: 14 August – Pakistan;15 August – India

1948 Jinnah died at Ziarat (11 September). War with India.

1951 First Constitution adopted on 19 February by the assembly, enforced on 28 March 1956. Assassination of Liaquat Ali Khan (16 October).

1958 – 1969 Martial Law regime; Field Marshal Ayub Khan. Abrogation of the Constitution of 1956. Imposition of Martial Law by Ayub Khan.

1961 Family Laws Ordinance restricts polygamy, regulates divorce and raises the marriageable age for girls to a minimum of 16.

1962 The new constitution of Pakistan.

1965 War with India over Raan of Kach.

1970 Elections. Pakistan Awami League successful in East Pakistan.

1971 Military action in East Pakistan. President Yahya Khan resigns and Zulfiqar Ali Bhutto becomes the President and Chief Marshal Law Administrator. Pakistan Army surrenders in Dhaka; Bangladesh born.

1973 New Constitution approved unanimously by the National Assembly 10 April.

1974 Ahmadis declared Non-Muslims.

1977 Elections. Martial Law imposed in certain areas. In July Prime Minister Zulfiqar Ali Bhutto arrested for alleged election rigging. General Mohammad Zia-ul-Haq took control and imposed Martial Law nationally.

1979 Promulgation of Hadood Ordinance, introducing so-called Islamic punishments for crimes including slander, theft, rape, adultery, fornication (*zina*) and prostitution.

1983 Women's demonstration against discriminatory laws, in Lahore. First street protest against Martial Law.

1984 Islamic Law of Evidence passed. The Law states that in matters relating to 'financial and future obligations' the evidence of two men or one man and two women will be required.

1985 General Mohammed Zia-ul-Haq lifts Martial Law. Number of women's seats raised to 20 in the National Assembly.

1986 Benazir Bhutto returns to lead the Pakistan People's Party and demands elections.

1988 Zia-ul-Haq dies in a plane crash in August. Elections held in November. Benazir Bhutto becomes Prime Minister in December.

1990 Ishaq Khan dissolves the National Assembly. Benazir Bhutto's government dismissed. Elections held. Nawaz Sharif takes over as the Prime Minister (October)

1993 Assembly dissolved again. Benazir Bhutto becomes the Prime Minister again.

Secession of East Pakistan

Events leading to the formation of Bangladesh date back to 1948, when Urdu was declared the official language of Pakistan, even though 56 per cent of the population spoke Bengali, the language of East Pakistan. Resentment among the people of East Pakistan increased as they felt economically and politically marginalised. The devastating cyclone that hit East Pakistan in 1970 and the Central Government's inability to respond adequately confirmed their perceptions. When the Central Government refused to accept the result of 1970 elections, it was the last straw: East Pakistan erupted with violent clashes between civilians and the army. A nine-month civil war followed, and the resulting exodus of refugees into India gave the Indian government a reason to intervene. The Indian Army entered East Pakistan in December 1971. After a brief resistance a UN-sponsored cease-fire was called on 17 December 1971 and the Pakistan Army surrendered. Pakistan was dismembered and the state of Bangladesh was born.

The Bhutto years (1971-77)

West Pakistan was governed by a Pakistan People's Party (PPP) government under Zulfiqar Ali Bhutto. His slogan had been 'Roti, kapra aur makaan' (food, clothing, and shelter) and his politics populist. There were great expectations of his government, on the part of the landless, trade unions, and left-wing political parties, and his home province of Sindh. His main opponents ranged from the far right to the far left, and included the political power holders in the provinces of Baluchistan and the Frontier, as well as the mullahs. An opposition coalition, the Pakistan National Alliance (PNA), led demonstrations and protest marches. Bhutto tried to placate them by passing token 'Islamic' legislation but at the same time declared martial law in certain areas. This paved the way for a complete military take-over, under General-Zia-ul-Haq, Bhutto's own Commander in Chief, chosen for his loyalty.

The Zia years (1977-88)

When Zia imposed Martial Law in 1977 his stated intentions were to restore order in the country and to hold elections within 90 days. But very soon his mission changed: to convert Pakistan into a truly Muslim state. Once again, Pakistan saw the banning of political activities. Summary courts sent scores of people to prison and the gallows, with no right of defence.

The non-elected military dictator General Zia was regarded as an international pariah, because of the hanging of Bhutto on a murder charge; but with the outbreak of the Afghan war, he suddenly became the courageous defender of a strategic frontier against communism. Military aid for the Afghan mujahideen and the obliging Pakistan government flowed in freely from Western governments and right-wing groups. Private militias grew and civil society rapidly became militarised. Ethnic, clan, and religio-sectarian rivalries flourished. Sindh, in particular became the scene of violent ethnic conflict between the native Sindhis and immigrant muhajirs.

Return to democracy

General Zia's death in August 1988 in a plane crash brought an end to a bleak phase of Pakistan's political life. But the transition to democracy has not been an easy one. In the five years between 1988 and 1993 three general elections were held, twice because of dismissals of elected governments by the President.

Political activity revived during the general election of 1988. The PPP leader, Benazir Bhutto, daughter of Zulfiqar Ali Bhutto, was elected Prime Minister. She became the first woman leader in the Muslim world, in recent times. The return to a civilian dispensation did not entirely reduce the influence of the military. The political deadlock between the three centres of power – the PM, the President, and the army – led to the dissolution of the assemblies by the President through extra constitutional powers, just 20 months after elections.

The 1990 elections, which were won by Nawaz Sharif and the Muslim League, were marred by the vehement allegations by the PPP that the elections had been rigged. The atmosphere in the new legislature remained tense. Once again, the assemblies were dissolved. October 1993 saw fresh elections, this time under the supervision of the army. The PPP and Benazir Bhutto were returned, but the electorate registered its protest by a low turnout. However, the marginal parties, particularly the religious, gained very few votes.

Benazir Bhutto

'When Bibi [the young lady] wins, will she be able to sit on the *gaddi* [seat]? Will she give it to her husband? Will he allow her to sit?' asked a peasant woman in disbelief in a village on the outskirts of Lahore during Benazir Bhutto's election campaign in 1988. Benazir, an Oxford graduate, had been forced into a two-year self-exile by the military government after spending five long years in prison and under house arrest. She returned on 10 April 1986 to a tumultuous welcome. Hundreds of thousands of people lined the streets of Lahore when she arrived. There was singing and dancing in the streets, and a feeling of euphoria. Her public meetings attracted mammoth crowds, including large numbers of women.

Benazir Bhutto's success in the elections and assumption of office as the Prime Minister vindicated people's belief in themselves, particularly women activists who had relentlessly challenged discriminatory laws and regulations. That, in a country where women are underprivileged, a woman, and a young one at that, could reach the highest public office, was extremely reassuring. It was clear that for the electorate gender was not the determining criteria for leadership. That she has disappointed people by her inability to keep electoral promises is another story.

Benazir Bhutto and her husband at their wedding.

Pakistan and its neighbours

The unsolved problem of the disputed territory of Kashmir has persistently soured relations between India and Pakistan, preventing them from co-operating in ways that would contribute to both countries' development. So far, relatively few refugees have fled Kashmir, and many of those that have come have dispersed into small settlements, or are living with relatives.

The American influence on Pakistan was most evident under the government of Ayub Khan 1958-68 and Zia-ul-Haq, particularly in 1971, when India had a military pact with the Soviet Union. Pakistan has also had a very special relationship with China, and helped to negotiate the first surprise talks between China and the US, considered to be a great diplomatic feat. Since the end of the Cold War, Pakistan has lost its strategic importance to the US as a means of keeping Afghanistan as 'Russia's bleeding wound'.

Pakistan has close links with most of the countries of the Middle East, but it is something of a love-hate relationship. Pakistani workers in the Middle East are often at the receiving end of harsh employment practices and social discrimination, and yet most Pakistanis were fiercely opposed to the government's participation in the war with Iraq, not wishing to be in what was clearly seen as the American camp against a major Muslim country; although Saudi Arabia, another powerful Muslim country, was also on the American side.

Links between Pakistan and Iran are strong, as neighbours and because of the Persian roots of the Urdu language. Large numbers of Iranians, students, refugees, and others, live in Pakistan, and there are also Persian-speaking Pakistani communities, mostly in Baluchistan. Many Pakistanis felt deeply involved with the Iranian struggle against the Shah. The Shi'a branch of Islam (see p.32)

NICK GARDNER

Unofficial camp for Afghan refugees, north of Quetta, near the Afghanistan border.

in Pakistan has strong links with Iran.

Of late, Pakistan has been developing trade, tourism, and cultural links with many of the Central Asian republics of the ex-Soviet Union, although the war in Afghanistan has somewhat constrained this relationship.

The Afghan War

During the Afghan War, Pakistan played host to three to four million Afghan refugees. The poor of both countries became the innocent victims of the Cold War; Afghans had to flee their homes, and Pakistanis had to cope with four million unexpected guests. With no end in sight to the internal conflicts in Afghanistan, Pakistan continues to pay a heavy price for its hospitality.

The majority of the refugees remained in camps in North West Frontier Province and Baluchistan, but a substantial number spread across the country, many of them settling in Karachi. The infusion of Afghans into an already polarised Pakistani society, and their ability to obtain arms and drugs from the war-torn border region, has created serious problems.

'The Kalashnikov culture'

Arms were channelled to the Afghan *mujahideen* by many Western countries, principally the US, to help them in their fight against Communism. Inevitably, many of these arms went astray and were sold, some to other governments, and many to the local Afghan and Pakistani population. Weapons of all descriptions, from small pistols to rocket launchers, SAMs, and landmines, are all readily available at bargain prices in the tribal areas of Pakistan, on the Afghan border. The inevitable result of this 'Kalashnikov culture' has been an increase in armed robberies, kidnappings for ransom, and gun-battles between rival groups.

The Pashtuns have always been a warrior people, and arms were manufactured in the town of Darra, but the most sophisticated weapon produced was a seven-shot rifle. Weapons such as this were used for celebratory firing at weddings when the groom was carrying off his bride. Now with the easy availability of Kalashnikovs (imitations are now being produced in Darra) a hail of Kalashnikov bullets are fired in the air at the departure of the bride and groom. What goes up must come down, and inevitably some of these bullets cause serious injury; a village organisation in Safiabad, Mardan, is campaigning to discourage people from this dangerous form of celebration.

Boring a gun barrel, in Darra, a town famous for the manufacture of weapons.

DAVE TOMSON

The drug culture

Another consequence of the Afghan influx has been the easy availability of heroin. Pakistan is not only used as a staging post for heroin smuggling, but a high cost has been paid in terms of the increased incidence of heroin addiction among the Pakistani population. In 1977 there were only 50 notified heroin addicts in Pakistan; now there at least one million or more.

The young man, his head shaven, was in the blue cotton uniform of the Centre, 'This is the second time I have come here', he said. 'I am the youngest in my family, I work in our photography shop in Quetta, with my brothers, and we are comfortably off. It was peer pressure made me try heroin: my friends taunted me for not using it. It makes you feel wonderful, but it destroys your life: you're no good for anything or anyone, family or work. My wife is fed up, and threatening to leave me. That's why I'm here again – it's my only hope, my last chance,'

What sets the Milo Centre apart from the many other drug clinics that have sprung up all over the country is the strong community involvement in its running, The building, in a busy street in Quetta, is fortified to keep addicts in and drug pushers out. The atmosphere is quiet and friendly. Timings for meals, exercise, collective discussions, TV watching, are carefully worked out and followed. The 25 patients on a one-month detoxification course are cared for by a team of doctors, who give their services free, Other volunteers work a shift system to support the handful of paid staff. Expenses are covered by contributions from patients and community donations.

The centre was set up by Milo Shaheed, who had been a local tough, but who was transformed into a crusader against heroin when his brother became an addict. He fought the drug pushers with courage and

energy until in 1990 one of them gunned him down at the gates of the clinic he had founded. But his commitment to rehabilitation of addicts and his fight against those who profit from heroin addiction has been an inspiration to those who continue his work today.

(above) **Patients at the Milo Centre.**

(below) **This passer-by discovered a heap of opium poppies left to dry by the roadside. Opium is grown in many areas of Afghanistan, and in some remote areas of Pakistan, although the government destroys crops when they are discovered, It is a high value crop, attractive to poor farmers.**

The school in the camp

For ten years, the Khairabad camp sprawled on the outskirts of Quetta: row upon row of small, mud-roofed huts, bleak and dusty, with no amenities. It was home to several thousand refugees. They were unregistered, and therefore had no official refugee status, and were not entitled to any material support. Many of them lived in home-made shelters of tattered cloth, even during the Quetta winter, with the snow piled high on the ground and temperatures below freezing.

The men either worked as day labourers in Quetta or were involved in the business of war. In 1991, the uneasy peace in Afghanistan offered a fragile hope to refugees, and the Khairabad camp quickly emptied. But less than a year later, most of them had been forced to return. The school building had been razed to the ground, but the camp leader, Agha Majeed and the teacher, Ghulam Rasool, were determined to restart a school.

A group of young volunteer teachers offered their help, many of them new refugees from Kabul. Latifa, for example, wanted her three young children to attend school, and offered to teach at the school herself. 'At least my children are having an education, and I am right here with them. They are delighted they have other children to play with. And they come and go from school in safety. In the last days before we left Kabul, we lived in constant terror.'

With no permanent site, the school moves every few months. The present school building has only one room, the rest of the children study packed into the tiny courtyard. There is not even a single blade of grass: 'There is not time to even plant a tree, before we are asked to move again by the landlord,' says Ghulam Rasool.

The 364 children in the school, 120 of whom are girls, pay a small fee, out of which the rent is paid for the school building, and the teachers share the tiny sum left over. But Latifa and the other teachers feel they must go on: 'Even if we could afford it, if we sent our children to Pakistani schools, they would have to study in a foreign language, and then how would they readjust to Afghan society? We are waiting for peace. Let peace come and we will be on our way home. I really need every penny I can earn, but this work is a labour of love, to ensure that our next generation does not grow up illiterate and uneducated. They are, after all, the future of Afghanistan.'

ZEHRA HASSAN

(facing page) **Afghan refugee children at the school in the Khairabad camp.**

(left) **Two of the young teachers in the school.**

Islam and Islamisation

Islam originated from the same part of the world as other great religions, the Middle East. Muslims believe that their Prophet Muhammad (peace be upon him) comes from the same line as Abraham, Moses, David, and Jesus, all of whom are recognised as prophets bringing the same message from the same God, Allah. The Muslims own the religious texts of the Torah, the Bible, and the Quran, as part of their tradition, and consider Jews and Christians as 'Ahl-e-Kitab', or 'people of the book'.

The basic affirmation of the Islamic faith is 'There is no God but the One God, Allah, and Muhammad is his prophet.' (La Ilaha Illa Allah, Muhammad ur Rasul Allah.) Muslims believe that Muhammad is the last prophet. The Muslims, however, are not homogeneous. The majority of Muslims in Pakistan are from the Sunni sect, which is further divided into many schools of thought. A significant minority belong to the Shi'a branch of Islam, also subdivided into *fiqah* or religious schools.

The schism among Muslims occurred in AD 658 over the succession to Muhammad, as the Caliph. The Sunnis believed that the Caliph should be chosen from the broader Muslim community, while the Shi'as believed that he should be a descendant of the Prophet. Through succeeding centuries, the Sunnis have come to represent the establishment, with religion closely identified with the state, and discouraged reinterpretations of Koranic law by scholars. Shi'a Islam has tended to be associated with new thought, radical movements, and more liberal interpretations of the rights of women. Sunni Islam is more closely identified with the keepers of the Ka'aba, the most sacred shrine of the Muslims, in Mecca, Saudi Arabia. The Shi'as have a strong concept of the clergy as spiritual leaders; while the Sunnis consider the clergy to be only religious scholars and administrators of the mosques.

People's Islam

While most Pakistanis (96.7 per cent) are Muslims, at its inception the country did not see itself as a religious or theocratic state, but as a place where people could practice their religion and pursue their lives without fear of discrimination and persecution. The proportion of Christians (1.6 per cent) is small and that of Hindus even smaller (1.5 per cent). Also present in Pakistan is a small but influential and controversial sect, the Ahmadis or Qadianis. The Ahmadis were declared non-Muslims in 1974 for not accepting the basic Islamic tenet that Prophet Muhammad is the last in the line of Prophets. The community since then has faced considerable persecution, especially during General Zia-ul-Haq's time, when stringent laws were passed against them.

People's religion is part of their personal lives – they perform rituals, celebrate festivals, commemorate auspicious days, visit *mazars* for mental peace, and enjoy devotional music. But the business of day-to-day living is governed by the practicalities and demands of the material world. Even social relationships are defined more by customary practices and cultural norms than by religion alone.

For most Pakistanis, Islam gives a sense of community and identity, an important one among other identities. It implies a moral and ethical code. It

Friday prayers, Karachi.

demands certain rituals: many Pakistani men (but by no means all) pray at the mosque on Fridays, and many more pray during the month of Ramazan. Most urban and many rural people fast during Ramazan. The two Eids are important celebrations. The festival of Eid ul Fitr is celebrated after the fast, and Eid ul Azha commemorates the sacrifice of Abraham, and is celebrated at the time thousands of pilgrims perform the pilgrimage in Mecca. Muslims who can afford it sacrifice an animal, and the meat is divided into three shares: one for the family, one for relatives and friends, and one for charity.

The vast majority of Pakistanis observe the prohibition of alcohol, although hashish and tobacco are more socially acceptable than in Western society. Marriage, death, and birth are surrounded by rituals, some religious, others social and cultural.

Outsiders to Islam often consider that women have a low status in Islam, but this view would not be shared by many Muslims. Views about women within Islam are as varied as views about women in any other context, ranging from the arch-conservative extreme to Feminist Islam, of which the Pakistani academic, Dr Riffat Hassan, is a prominent example. Pakistan boasts a woman Prime Minister, women pilots, women taxi-drivers, and women in every sphere of life; as well as women who are locked within the *chadar* (veil) and the *chardivari* (the four walls of the home); they are all Muslim women.

State Islam

Part of Pakistan's particular brand of political development has been the transition from people's Islam to state Islam. Over the years Islam has become central to the political life of the country, often used as a legitimising tool for unpopular governments, unpopular actions, and new social movements. Muslim identity, the primary unifying factor for the citizens of Pakistan, has been exploited by the religious right.

Initially, this was not taken seriously by the non-theocratic leadership, who believed that a liberal, democratic political system was well within the parameters of an Islamic state.

The political use of Islam increased mainly because of the lack of consensus among political elites, as a way of gaining support from religious groups. In the process, the latter began to play a more critical role in political affairs. Under Zia's leadership, the politicisation of religion increased, because he had no electoral mandate for his continued rule.

When Zia came to power, Iran was engaged in a violent struggle with its Shah, who was propped up by the US; Afghanistan was on the brink of its holy war with the communists; Pakistan had been through its honeymoon with capitalism under Ayub Khan, and its populist socialist rhetoric and paralysing 'nationalisation' policy under Bhutto. The political context was ripe for a third way, specific to Pakistan.

Although few held fundamentalist views, most Pakistanis gave tacit support to whatever was cited in the name of Islam, not realising the lengths to which the religion would be exploited and the level of prescriptiveness that the government would introduce. Religion was seen as a family and personal matter, and Islam had been interpreted and practised in a thousand different ways. Only under a totalitarian government could certain options be declared unacceptable, and a single fundamental text proclaimed to which everyone must conform.

Zia's rule marked the coming together of the obscurantists' world view with that of the state. The religious parties, who before and since never fared well in elections, were for the first time part of the state machinery, in positions of power, and able to procure advantages for themselves. Land and money was now easily available for religious schools (*madarasahs*), religious groups were recruited in *zakat* committees, to allocate compulsory religious taxes, they entered the media, educational institutions, and trade unions.

Even after the restoration of democracy, and the repeated electoral rejection of religious parties by the people, the rhetoric of 'Islamisation' continues. The influence of politicised religion is so strong that every subsequent government feels bound to demonstrate its commitment.

However, it has been most interesting for Pakistanis to observe, in view of the West's paranoia about Islamic fundamentalism, that, in many cases, fundamentalists have received the full backing of Western countries, when it suited their purposes. The *mujahideen* were allies in fighting Communism in Afghanistan; and General Zia-ul-Haq, standard-bearer of state Islam, received generous American aid; the Saudi government, with its own brand of Islamic fundamentalism, was an acceptable ally during the war with Iraq.

Among the legislation enacted in the name of Islam are the Ordinance against the Ahmadis and a Blasphemy Law. The former makes Ahmadis liable to punishment for referring to themselves as Muslims and to their places of prayers as 'mosques', or making public calls for prayers (*azaan*). The Blasphemy Law covers derogatory statements about Prophet Muhammad. The prescribed penalty is death. These two laws have led to extensive victimisation. Since the Blasphemy Law is very vague and ambiguous about the content of derogatory remarks it has been repeatedly invoked to settle personal or political scores. To try cases under Islamic Law, a parallel judiciary, the Federal Shariat Court, was created. The PPP government has expressed its intention to review the laws introduced by General Zia-ul-Haq, but currently none have been repealed.

Could Pakistan become another Iran or Algeria? The links of Pakistan's religious militants with those abroad is a cause for concern. But despite the capacity of the religious parties to bring pressure on

**The Faisal Mosque,
Islamabad.**

government, to stop traffic or to shut
markets, the over-riding fact is that these
parties have not succeeded in increasing
their popular vote nor their presence in
parliament. For most people the feeling
for Islam is very strong but equally
strong is their rejection of those who
would define Islam for them, or are seen
to be using Islam to further their own
vested political interests.

Women and Zia's policies

There is no question that the 'Islamisation' package designed by Zia and his political allies was singularly damaging to women. But it must be stressed that Zia's definition of Islamisation was extremely controversial, essentially a layman's uneducated opinion, and has been widely criticised by the extreme right, by Islamic scholars, and by progressive schools of thought in Islam.

The first Islamisation legislation was the Hudood Ordinances (1979). These cover theft, drunkenness, adultery, rape, and bearing false witness, and prescribe maximum punishment for each. Under this law, women's evidence is not permissible for maximum (*hadd*) punishment, though for lesser punishments (*tazeer*) it may be admissible. The most serious aspect of the law is that it does not make a distinction in the level of proof required for the crimes of adultery (*zina*) and rape (*zina-bil-jabr*). To conclusively prove either, four male Muslim eye-witnesses of good repute are required. The equating of adultery with rape has had extremely negative implications for women. Innumerable women, particularly the uneducated and underprivileged, have been imprisoned on false charges, or flogged, under this law, while the perpetrators of the crime of rape have escaped punishment.

The Law of Evidence (1984) requiring 'The evidence of two men, or one man and two women so that if one should forget, the other may remind her' in financial transactions, unless the woman is appearing in an official capacity (Article 17), had similar negative implications, even if in reality the law is rarely invoked. It establishes a stereotype of women as mentally inferior, unreliable and inconsistent

A number of directives were issued by Zia, regarding the dress code, gender segregation, campaigns against obscenity, covering of the head by female announcers on TV, banning of sports for women, a separate university for women, an end to foreign postings of women in the foreign service, and limiting women's recruitment in banks and other public services. Not all these measures were implemented; the dress code, for example, has never been enforced.

DAVE TOMSON

Women from the conservative branch of Islam wear enveloping veils in public places.

Resisting Extremism

There are two mosques in the small village of Goth Janano, one for Sunnis and one for Shi'as. Six Hindu families also live in the village. There is considerable potential for religious tensions, but local community leaders are dedicated to resolving any conflicts and keeping communication open between people of different sects and faiths.

'In the last days of Muharram there's a lot of grief and sorrow,' says Muhammed Buksh, one of the village leaders. 'This is when we relive the death of the grandson of the Prophet. During this time we have a session of mourning every evening. At this time even the Hindus join us, which helps to bind the community together.

'I want to share a fear of mine with you: every Friday, outside speakers from the Shi'a and Sunni sects come to the village and talk at the mosques. I have encouraged a Sunni and a Shi'a to get elected on to our village committee, so that they have to work together and achieve positive things. I've organised other committees so that both sects have to work together, one on health, one on registering births and deaths, and so on. If we can't stop it [i.e. the divisions being created by outsiders] getting out of hand, things will get in a real mess.

'We're working to stem the tide. We are having a series of lectures in the village at the moment about human development: when people started living in communities, building houses, and so on, to show that we are all the same.'

Every village in Pakistan, however small and remote, has its own mosque. The mosque is not only a place of worship but acts as the social centre of village life. This mosque is in a village in southern Punjab.

LIZ CLAYTON

37

Economy and development

Pakistan might have become one of the Asian success stories. It is potentially a prosperous country, with the resources to save all its current population from poverty. But this potential has not been realised, and according to the UN's 1992 *Human Development Report*, 36 million people subsist below the poverty line.

Considering that Pakistan had no industrial base to speak of when it came into existence, nor a highly developed infrastructure, its economic progress has been remarkable. Relatively liberal economic policies, together with the industry and thrift of its people, and a helping hand from foreign aid, have led to steady economic growth. GNP growth rate has increased to about 6-7 per cent per annum during the 1980s, doubling since 1972. The annual per capita income of US$400 is the second highest in South Asia after Sri Lanka. Pakistan has managed to keep its economic growth rate ahead of its bounding population growth rate of 3.1 per cent. Pakistan is not over-dependent on primary commodity exports, and has succeeded in diversifying its exports, with textiles forming the largest element. Over the past two decades, Pakistan has benefited from a valuable form of export: its manpower. Remittances form migrant workers, particularly from the Gulf, played a major role in keeping the economy booming during the 1970s and 1980s.

Winnowing grain. Although agriculture in some parts of Pakistan is highly sophisticated and mechanised, in the more remote areas traditional farming methods are still in use.

ZEHRA HASSAN

Primarily, Pakistan's is a rural economy. The agricultural sector accounts for about 26 per cent of GDP and for 47 per cent of total employment. It contributes the most to the country's earnings (rice and cotton exports) – about 60 per cent between 1984 and 1990. The industrial sector, on the other hand, accounts for about 25 per cent of GDP, employing 22 per cent of the labour force; and the service sector 49 per cent, providing employment to 33 per cent. The industrial and service sectors are a mix of public and private enterprises.

A major source of foreign exchange earnings has been the high level of remittances from Pakistan's workers abroad. Although on the decline these are still about US$1.75 billion, which is equal to about a quarter of total export earnings or 3.7 per cent of GNP. Total export earnings amount to 16 per cent of GDP (all figures from *Human Development Report*, 1994).

Debt

Although not classed as a severely indebted country, Pakistan is dependent on external borrowing. In 1991-92 the interest on both economic and foreign debt went up by 31 per cent; the total external debt then amounting to US$23bn. This works out at about £125 owed per Pakistani, and some 21 per cent of Pakistan's export revenues go towards servicing this debt. Payment of interest works out at £4.50 for each Pakistani. Over the years, debt servicing and high military expenditure has made the economy more and more dependent on foreign resources. For this reason, the International Monetary Fund (IMF) asked Pakistan to implement a programme of structural reforms in its economy. The government has had to commit itself to increased taxes, reduced public spending and reduced price subsidies, so that the government deficit falls substantially. This, as in other developing countries, has led to inflation, spiralling prices, and harsh living conditions for low-income groups.

Pakistan is a country with a strong military tradition, and joining the army or an unofficial militia is a recognised way of earning a living.

Military expenditure

Pakistan's military expenditures are high (6.5 per cent of its GDP), the equivalent of Rs.556 per person. Pakistan justifies high spending by the perceived security threat from India and the latter's spending on defence. (India's military expenditure is substantial, with 12 per cent of all its imports comprising non-nuclear arms.) Pakistan received a spurt of US-sponsored military aid following the 1979 USSR intervention in Afghanistan.

Underdevelopment in Pakistan

The dominant forces in the political economy since Partition have been the feudal elites of Punjab and Sindh, the army, the bureaucracy, and the bourgeoisie. These dominant political elites have been able to divert the bulk of public spending away from poverty alleviation and social services. This process is most visible in the way that the armed forces have appropriated the lion's share of state resources. Interest payments on government debt have also been high. The result is that little revenue is left for improving water supply, health care, or educational facilities, or for other social priorities. Each year the Pakistan government (federal and provincial combined) spends Rs 164 on Education and a paltry Rs 78 on health per capita.

Pakistan has failed to provide many of its people with the basic necessities of life, despite the availability of resources. The roots of this failure lie in the political structures and the development model that has been adopted. Pakistan's bureaucratically-regulated, free-market strategy has allowed incomes to grow but there has been little investment in basic services, and social inequalities have increased. In comparison with its south Asian neighbours, Pakistan's average income is only rivalled by Sri Lanka, but its achievements in education, health care, and provision of water are way behind Sri Lanka and India and are barely on a par with poorer countries like Bangladesh and Nepal.

Profile of poverty in Pakistan

Poverty in Pakistan involves more than lack of food or basic necessities. Among the 36 million poor people are groups who are economically, socially, and politically marginalised; they lack productive assets with which to earn a living, they are despised or neglected by their community, and they lack political or legal protection. People such as landless labourers, tenant farmers, and marginal farmers are among the poorest in Pakistan; in urban areas, the poorest are those who do not own any property, renting even the shack they live in. Religious minorities, such as the Punjabi Christians and the Sindhi Hindus, are among the poorest people in Pakistan. The most vulnerable of all are the 'untouchable' castes, looked down on by fellow Hindus and Muslims.

Many women in Pakistan are restricted in their mobility, education, and services, and economic participation, and many experience domestic violence. They are often discriminated against in the distribution of household resources, and by the legal system. Women-headed households are a small but particularly vulnerable group. However, not all women are equally disadvantaged: women from the middle classes, who are generally educated, are in a better position to defend themselves.

Bonded workers are often exploited by their employers in what amounts to a latter-day form of slavery. The bondage arises from a loan taken by the worker from the money lender, who may be a rich trader in his village, or the owner of a factory. Bonded labour, in its classic form, is most common at the brick kilns, but is also found in other rural and urban occupations. The indebted workers are unable to leave their employer, unless they find another employer willing to pay off their loan (in effect, to buy them). They are forced to accept very low wages, from which there are systematic deductions for debts, and to work in poor conditions. Often the whole family provides the labour, normally at piecework rates.

Rural workers, agricultural or artisan, are also very often effectively bonded. To buy household necessities, they get into debt with the village shop-keeper. They are then bound to sell all their produce to him at a rate that is well below the market price, at the same time as paying prohibitive rates of interest on the loan. Floods, illnesses, and the like can put a family in bondage for life.

Child labour

Children in the families of bonded labourers suffer particularly, as they help to pay off a loan taken by their parents. They are deprived of education, and poor working conditions and sexual harassment may scar them for life. Child labour can be found in almost every sector, but is most common in carpet weaving, the brick kilns, and small-scale manufacturing, such as shoe-making. In one of the Bengali Burmese immigrant settlements on the outskirts of Karachi

family took out a loan of Rs6,000 (£124) when Razia's father first fell ill in late 1993. Today, half their pay goes in *peshgi,* that is, towards paying off the loan. That's £1.14 every day for more than two years – and no sign of the payments ever coming to an end. Says Razia: 'All we get is weeping and wailing about money.'

(left) **Bricks drying in the sun.**

(below) **Razia making bricks.**

Razia's story

Razia's family lives and works at a *bhatta* (brick kiln) outside Lahore. In 1994 her father died, leaving nine-year-old Raiza, her younger brothers and sisters, her mother and grandparents. To survive, they must make at least 1,000 bricks a day. They are paid per brick, and lose money for every one that is damaged. Razia's grandmother is too old to work making bricks, so she stays at home and looks after the small children. Razia's grandfather still helps to make bricks, but he has asthma, so he can only make about 50 bricks a day. That means that Razia and her mother have to make the rest, and do all the housework. There's more to it than just making the bricks, they must mix the clay and dry the bricks as well – the bricks must be turned so that they dry evenly before they are fired, each side must face the sun for half a day. For their 1,000 bricks, the family is paid Rs110 (about £2.28). The

small carpet workshops are the mainstay of impoverished families, who pledge their children's labour for loans to build houses or meet other pressing expenses. One such workshop has 500 children working, some just five years old (*Newsline*, October 1993). The work environment is oppressive – low ceilings, and no ventilation. Their earnings usually go to parents who may have to use the money for daily expenses and not always for repaying the initial loan.

Child labour of this sort is a complex issue to tackle. Banning it without clear alternatives may even be counter-productive, pushing children, sometimes sole earners for their families, into even worse situations of exploitation, such as prostitution. Multi-pronged action at different levels is what is required – a combination of literacy and alternative skills for the children and employment opportunities for parents. Some NGOs offer education and literacy to children outside working hours. But these are few and far between, and there are many thousands of child workers in Pakistan.

The Carpet Weavers

'Why don't you send your sons to school?' I asked the mother of six boys in one of Lahore's slums. Abandoned by her husband, she lives in an illegal one-room lean-to not far from the main railway station. Her eldest son is in his twenties, the youngest 8 or 9 years old. Two of her sons, 12 and 15 years of age, are working in a home-based carpet weaving workshop. Her answer was simple. She had put the boys in a government school where after the first two or three grades the treatment by teachers become so harsh that they began to run away from school. Instead they would sneak off to the canal, swim and have a good time.

So she placed them in the workshop. 'At least I know where they are, and they are learning a skill and getting free food. Above all, I do not have to kill myself with anxiety over their getting into bad company, taking drugs or drowning in the canal!' Once they are proficient at weaving they will bring in much needed income. As many hands as possible have to earn.

The informal sector

The informal sector includes everything from small-scale manufacturing to road-side tea stalls. Statistics are not reliable, but huge numbers of men, women and children are involved. Workers in this sector are often extremely poor. One of the side-effects of Pakistan's relatively stringent labour laws has been for large-scale manufacturers to 'put out' work to women working at home, and to small workshops employing fewer than ten

Young boy working in a carpet weaving workshop. His earnings make a vital contribution to his family's survival.

BEN BUXTON

Street stall, selling a wide variety of goods.

(below) **This roadside leatherworker is carrying out a quick repair on the handle of the photographer's briefcase.**

workers, because these workers are not covered by the laws. Even multinational companies, such as shoe manufacturers, are now getting products made in these tiny workshops. In the garment industry, many larger units will employ people for just less than the statutory 90 days, lay them off for a week, and re-employ them again, to keep them perpetually short-term workers, who are legally unable to unionise. Food, sports goods, medical instruments, 70 per cent of textiles, and all carpets, are produced in small-scale workshops. The level of technology used and the wages paid are low; costs in the informal sector are only one-tenth of those of large-scale enterprises.

A great many women work in the informal economy. Because women whose mobility is restricted can only work at home, they are unable to organise, and not in a position to bargain, and so are liable to be exploited. The sheer pressure to survive is pushing more and more women into the labour force.

Scenes from middle-class life:
(above) Off to (private) school in a tonga.

(below) Enthusiastic audience at a pop concert.

The swelling middle class

Pakistan's industrial take-off in the 1960s triggered the formation of a middle class. By the 1990s this has emerged as a vibrant section of society. A combination of state patronage and their business acumen has propelled this new rich class to the centre stage where it is now aspiring for political power. The class is most visible in urban centres, expressing its new found affluence through ostentatious consumerism. It also seeks to lead the way in redefining existing cultural, political, social and economic identities and relationships.

The obvious prosperity of the middle class has led to the oft repeated comment that 'the people of Pakistan are prosperous but the government bankrupt'. State institutions and bureaucracy are becoming moribund: security is inadequate, electricity and water supply mismanaged, the telephone service non-functional. This is being compensated for by private security firms, private electricity generators, tube-wells in people's gardens, and payment for water brought by tankers.

Mobile phones, fashion shows, private English schools, burger joints with American-style menus, jeans, MTV music, permed hair, 'White House' architecture, huge weddings and parties, are some of the more ostentatious manifestations of the wealth of this new generation of Pakistan's upper-crust yuppies. The status of women within this social class is variable; some study abroad in the West, others are in purdah. Many middle-class women are highly visible, taking an active part in social activities; others are 'queens of their home'.

The emergence of the middle class has sharpened the differences between rural and urban areas, propelling rural-urban migration, as well as creating disparities between different regions and provinces. Clashes may occur in future in Pakistan between the old and the new elites. Benazir Bhutto's government and that of Nawaz Sharif, have sometimes been seen to epitomise this cultural divide, Bhutto representing the old feudals and Sharif the newly-emerging capitalists. Other commentators believe that the old feudals are turning into the new capitalists, with the sons of tenant farmers being recruited as labourers in the factory of the feudal lord.

Women in a changing society

Women in Pakistan play a major economic role that often goes unrecognised. In rural areas, in addition to their household tasks, poor women are active in agriculture, horticulture, animal husbandry, water carrying, and firewood gathering. At harvest time, thousands of women work on the land, many as cotton pickers. The construction sector traditionally employs the greatest number of woman labourers. Women are also fairly well represented in the service sectors of education, health, and administration.

The life of a Pakistani woman – like that of a Pakistani man – is determined by the social system, region, or class that she belongs to. She may be a peasant woman working from dawn to dusk in the fields alongside the men in her family, or providing unpaid family labour in a brick kiln. She may be leading a cloistered existence in a lower-middle-class urban neighbourhood, or be a highly-trained professional government or business executive.

Women are least visible in Baluchistan and NWFP, where social codes are very rigid. Some women in these two provinces are closely guarded and can even lose their life if suspected of contact with a male outside the immediate family. However, in parts of the Frontier-Kohistan region where tribal feuds are prevalent, women cultivate the land, while men remain indoors. In Punjab and Sindh, seclusion is relatively less stringent, and women work outdoors. They retain stronger links with their parental homes and families after marriage.

In the cities the pace of change is more rapid. Schools (both private and public), professional training, and higher education institutions, offer numerous opportunities to women. Women work in banks and administrative offices; as doctors, architects, and accountants; as industrial workers; and as entrepreneurs running businesses. There is a growing demand for women as secretaries, administrators, and computer operators. Large numbers of women work in small workshops, or in home-based production.

MARYAM IQBAL

PIA

Two extremes of women's life-styles in Pakistan: *(above)* **spreading a fresh layer of mud on the floor of a courtyard in preparation for a wedding;** *(below)* **the first two women pilots to be trained by the Pakistan International Airline.**

Despite their different life-situations, Pakistani women share a common disadvantage. There is a negative attitude to women within society: they have no identity of their own; they have limited access to economic or social power; they are seen as a burden, and also a symbol of the honour of the household, or a threat to it. Women are viewed as subordinate, as incapable of taking decisions, as dependants. The great majority are illiterate, weak in health, burdened by frequent childbirth. It is the patriarchal system of society in Pakistan which determines attitudes towards women. The system predates Islam and is embedded in the feudal and the pre-feudal tribal systems prevailing in different parts of the country. Patriarchal values pervade all strata of society, though there may be variations by class and region. However, the system is beginning to be challenged.

A moment of confrontation during the demonstration in Lahore against the Law of Evidence.

WOMEN'S ACTION FORUM

Women's resistance

The 1980s witnessed an intense mobilising of women to challenge discriminatory laws. Within months of each other, two new groups were set up: the Women's Action Forum, and Sindhiani Tehrik (Sindhi Women's Movement). The former represented continuity with earlier women's struggles, and was composed mainly of middle- and upper-middle-class women, whereas the Sindhiani Tehrik was the first rural women's organisation in the country. The platform of Women's Action Forum was rejection of the Hudood Ordinances, the Law of Evidence, and other religiously-motivated legislation, and of attempts to segregate universities. Negative images of women on the official media, their stereotyping according to prescribed roles (wife and mother) were vehemently opposed as distortions of reality. Street agitations, pickets, press campaigns, lobbying, research and writing forced politicians and government to recognise women as a political reality. Political parties and trade unions alike put women's issues on their agendas, and the government claimed that it was seriously concerned about women's welfare.

The paradoxes in Pakistani society will remain for a long time to come. What better example of this paradox than the fact that a woman could be elected as head of government – in a society which devalues its women by declaring that a woman's evidence is worth half that of a man's?

Women's militancy

In 1983, in Lahore, women organised a protest against the proposed Law of Evidence, in response to a call from a group of women lawyers. The plan was to march to the Punjab High Court and present a memorandum against the proposed law to the Chief Justice on behalf of women's organisations.

About 300 women from different walks of life – teachers, students and factory workers – gathered in a side street ... They were quite surprised to see a large number of male and female police in the area (at least 500 of them)... The women were told that they could not go to the High Court as that would be a violation of the law ... The women's assurances that they would walk in pairs with enough distance between them so as not to violate the law ... was not accepted by the duty magistrate... When force was used to remove from the scene Habib Jalib, an anti-government poet [who] recited poems specially written in support of women... enraged women broke through the police cordon and started running in the direction of the High Court.

A free-for-all followed. Groups of women zigzagged down the 40-ft wide Mall Road with police brandishing batons... some women were trapped by the police, beaten up, dragged along the road and rounded up into police vans. In the middle of it all tear gas was used... and the Mall Road presented a bizarre sight of a group of all-female demonstrators involved in a street fight with the police. Fifty women were arrested, but many managed to get to the High Court where male lawyers were waiting with garlands to receive them.
(Extracts from K. Mumtaz and F. Shaheed, *Women of Pakistan: Two Steps Forward One Step Back?*)

Female literacy

Poor people in Pakistan view education as an investment they make in their child's future. Education is regarded as a 'qualification' for a better job. One of the effects has been that people saw little reason to educate their daughters, since 'we are not sending our girls out to feed us, are we?' Education was seen as irrelevant for women, who were only going to work in the fields as unpaid family labourers, or as housewives.

This view is gradually changing. Nowhere in Pakistan is there a girls' school which is not packed with students. But there are many villages without a school for girls, and many girls' schools are understaffed and poorly equipped. What has not changed, or only for the worse, is the political will

of the government to provide primary education for all children, boys and girls; nor has the quality of the education provided improved.

In Pakistan there are hundreds of one-room private schools all over the country catering for the millions of children whose parents pay fees to get them an education. But there are also many drop-outs, children who run away from ill-treatment at the hands of teachers, or out of boredom with the education on offer. Among the poor, where a mother goes out to work, often the eldest daughter has to take her place in the home, and this may mean taking her away from school.

Yung girls learning the Koran, in the courtyard of a house in a village in Sindh.

Young student at the Nai Raushni Centre.

Nai Raushni (New Light) Centre, Quetta

There are little girls, not so little girls, and young and older women milling all over this building in the evenings. Over 200 students, from 12-year-olds to women in their forties, attend the Nai Raushni Centre in Quetta, making it the largest literacy and education centre for young girls and women in the country.

Fatima is a student here. A shy, quiet girl of 13, Fatima is the daughter of a day labourer, one of eight children. None of her brothers and sisters go to school. Two brothers are apprenticed to motorcycle mechanics, another works in a cobbler's shop, while the eldest works in a carpet factory. Fatima used to work in the carpet factory too, but earned so little that her mother went to work there instead, while Fatima stayed at home to cook and clean and look after her baby sisters. Fatima doesn't enjoy housework, but she was grateful to be spared the back-breaking carpet work.

In the evening Fatima's brothers go to the Nasl-e-nau Talimi Markaz, a literacy centre for working boys and men. One evening, they discovered that there was a similar centre for women, which did not run quite so late. Fatima was really excited and asked her mother if she could attend. Her mother made enquiries and came to see the teachers. Now Fatima goes there every evening, after her mother has returned home from work.

Fatima has an ambition: 'I would like to do my school-leaving exam and then become a teacher, so that I can teach other children who could not go to school,' she says. And with the help of Nai Raushni, she may well do so.

Bounding population

Pakistan's population growth rate at 3.1 per cent per annum is one of the highest in the world, making it the ninth most populous country. The population in the area which is now Pakistan was 16.5 million in 1901; it is currently about 120 million (with 45 per cent of the population below the age of 15 years) and is projected to double by the year 2017 if growth continues at the present rate.

The rapid increase in population has stretched the country's limited resources. There are not enough schools, health facilities or houses. The average number of people living in a house is seven; and half the population live in one-room housing units. Other basic utilities are also lacking: electricity is available to only 31 per cent of households; water and sanitation to very few people; and according to UNICEF estimates, only 55 per cent of the total population and 35 per cent of the rural population lives within 5km from a fixed health facility . There is a clear correlation between poverty and population. A study of a district in Punjab found that the landless had more children than those with large landholdings; that households where children contributed to labour had more children; and that, whereas the total fertility rate of the village was 6.1, the average number of living children was three. It appears that general poverty and economic insecurity create the need for more children in order to increase the earning capacity of the family.

The desire for large families is partly due to high levels of infant and child mortality. Few women dare to use irreversible methods of contraception after two or three children, given the high rates of mortality, a rate highest for the poorest parents.

Women's status in society is yet another factor in population growth. The preference for male children means that a woman's status increases with the number of male progeny she produces. One of the most profound forms of oppression endured by Pakistani women is excessive childbearing, due to lack of control over their fertility. Even women who do not want more children are unable to use contraceptives because of family pressure.

There is a widespread misapprehension that the use of contraceptives is in conflict with religion. While conservative social values and a particular interpretation of Islam lead many men to deny their wives the right to use birth control, there has been little serious government commitment to overcoming the problem.

MARYAM IQBAL

Sherbano and some of her grandchildren. Her sons live with her and help on the family farm. Having a large family is a way of ensuring that a woman will be cared for in her old age.

Kesro (centre, leaning on stick) and some of his descendants. The extended family is an integral part of Pakistan society.

Family-planning policy

Pakistan's is one of the oldest family planning programme in South Asia and it is also probably the least successful. Government policy on population planning has varied. For example, during General Zia-al-Haq's years of Martial Law, the number of field staff in the Population Department was drastically reduced. Family planning policy was officially 'reborn' in 1980, and for the first time a multisectoral approach emphasising the incorporation of Mother and Child Health Care, and the enhancement of education and employment opportunities, for women, was adopted. These inter-linkages have remained only a paper commitment as far as the government is concerned.

It is clear that the problem of rapid population growth will not be solved simply by providing services. Complex factors are involved: social norms placing a high value on sons, religious beliefs, unemployment, quality of health facilities, medical technologies, economic security, women's lack of education and status in society, their autonomy, and reproductive health rights. By and large, official policy has failed to recognise these factors. Because of the implicit assumptions that the biological function of reproduction can be divorced from the social context, and that women have the sole responsibility for bearing and rearing children, the focus of all family-planning programmes is on women, despite the fact that they are not in a position to make decisions or enforce their choices.

In recent years, however, a change in social mores is becoming apparent. More girls are attending school, particularly in rural areas, and the average age of marriage for girls has gone up from 17 years in 1981 to 20.2 years in 1993-1994. The correlation between improved female education and fertility rate is being recognised by policy makers (women with secondary education have on average 3.6 births per woman as opposed to an average of 5.7 births for women with no education).

There is a huge unmet need for birth control in Pakistan. According to the latest survey, only 18 per cent of married couples use contraception. The corresponding figures for Bangladesh and India are two and three times that figure. A good quality, readily available family-planning service could make a progressive and liberating contribution to development in Pakistan. It should be stressed that female circumcision is unknown in Pakistan. There is a widespread misunderstanding about this among foreigners.

Many women in Pakistan are in very poor health; as many as 90 per cent of pregnant and lactating women are anaemic. Restrictions on their mobility makes it difficult for them to get to a health facility or family planning service, and the burden of daily chores leaves them little time to seek such services.

In addition, services are of poor quality, and there is often a failure to provide women with proper counselling. Accounts of the unpleasant side-effects of a particular method can deter other potential users of contraceptives. Not only are health and family planning services inadequate in terms of coverage, but they lack facilities for follow-up, and there is an acute shortage of trained staff.

Health services in Pakistan

In Pakistan, only 56 per cent of people have safe drinking water, and just 24 per cent have good sanitation. Out of every 1000 babies born, 91 die before their first birthday. In Pakistan there are health services – doctors and health centres – for only 55 per cent of the population.

Non-government organisations have long been active in the health sector, ranging from flourishing national organisations, such as the Family Planning Association, to local charities running free dispensaries for poor people. At partition, Pakistan inherited a number of Mission Hospitals, which have been maintained, and several of them run community health projects. The Rosary Hospital, Gujrat, runs one such programme, the Community Health and Development Programme (CHDP).

Every day, hundreds of patients from the surrounding villages make the journey to the Rosary Hospital. Often, they come only at a very late stage of an illness, or when a woman is experiencing complications in labour. Staff at the hospital realised that some problems would be easier to tackle at an earlier stage, and that simple preventive measures could reduce the incidence of illness.

About ten years ago, the hospital started an outreach programme (CHDP) of health education, to give people information about immunisation, simple treatments for diarrhoea, the dangers of unregulated use of drugs, and other basic information. In the villages, they came face to face with the many other, inter-related problems with which poor people have to struggle. They realised that health education alone was inadequate, as there were so many other factors affecting women's lives and health.

'We would be lecturing them about the use of oral rehydration solution for infant diarrhoea, when they were worried to death about a husband who was becoming addicted to drugs, or how to raise a dowry for their daughter,' said Shakila, the leader of the CHDP team. So they have adapted traditional folk theatre techniques to talk about health education messages and about social problems such as dowry, and arranged marriages. The use of drama, song, music, and dance has proved a highly effective part of CHDP's work. They have also helped to run a small credit and savings scheme, encouraged children to clean up the environment and plant trees, helped villages to build latrines, and trained teachers for adult literacy classes.

Rational drugs policy

Of equal importance as the availability of health services is the treatment and the cost. As in many countries, a profusion of medicines are available over the counter. Not all are safe; many are of no benefit at all. The Network, an information and campaigning organisation, based in Islamabad, is tackling the problem.

'In Pakistan, what is not widely known is that we have an official essential drugs list,' says Dr Zafar, Director of The Network. 'We have published it in our newsletter, so that people are getting to know about it. We hold seminars for young doctors, giving them presentations on various aspects of rational drugs; in the next two years we will be covering all the medical colleges in Pakistan. We are also running

Dr Zafar, Director of The Network and campaigner for the rational use of drugs.

workshops for journalists and NGO health workers, giving them information about all these issues. Having good will is one thing, but people also need the basic knowledge. We tell them that you have to concentrate on essential drugs, and not waste your money on buying useless drugs. The rational prescribing of essential drugs is the next step.

'We thought we should work in a phased manner, starting at the policy level and the medical community. Going directly to the consumers needs a lot of resources, and a different kind of approach, which we are preparing ourselves for. In a country like Pakistan, if you can get a problem drug deregistered, that means you have saved millions of potential users of that drug.

'There is a study which shows that of the average household budget, 90 per cent of spending on health is spent on drugs; so there is a need to educate people. People think there is a pill for every illness. Instant cure! People spend very little on preventive care, hygiene, cleanliness, and check-ups.

'There is a clear conflict of interest with the pharmaceutical companies, but I always start my presentations with a positive note: no modern health care system can survive without drugs. The question is, what kind of drugs? Around 30 per cent of all the drugs manufactured in Pakistan are tonics and vitamins, which are absolutely useless; another 50 per cent are non-essential drugs, which are heavily promoted by the industry to doctors.

'Now the pharmaceutical companies know we are here, and we have started affecting public opinion, and they see us as a group which is going to stay and which has legitimate concerns, so they'd better take us seriously.'

Pakistan's environmental problems

Pakistan, like a number of other developing countries, is faced by two mutually reinforcing crises: the seemingly persistent problem of poverty, and environmental destruction. Pakistan is not a major producer of CFC-gases or emitter of greenhouse gases, does not contribute to the global environmental crisis, but remains vulnerable to both the threat of climate change and depletion of the ozone layer. Like other developing countries, it is suffering a loss of bio-diversity: animal and plant species known to have existed in the past have vanished, and many more are under threat of extinction. The expansion of human settlements and unlawful hunting practices have reduced the numbers of animals such as the ibex, snow leopard, wildass, and houbara bustard to danger level, and a number of plant species are disappearing fast. The imbalance in the ecological order has long-term effects: for example, the number of snakes has decreased, and as a result rat numbers have in increased greatly, causing heavy grain losses.

Natural resources are being misused; only half of the urban excreta is disposed in sewers; hazardous chemicals are disposed of in water-ways and other convenient places like empty lots; motor vehicles emit deadly fumes; land is being lost to desertification, waterlogging and soil erosion; there is destruction and degradation of forests; wetlands are being drained; the food-chain is being poisoned.

The roots of these problems are economic and demographic pressures on a limited resource base, and the failure to manage natural resources sustainably. Regulatory measures are inadequate, or, more often, not strictly applied.

Government departments lack co-ordination and are unable to deal with cross-sectoral issues. There is also a preference for large infrastructural projects, like the Left Bank Outfall Drain to deal with waterlogging, the Tarbela Dam, and the proposed Kalabagh Dam.

Water is a vital natural resource, for which demand is constantly rising. A

Headwater control point on the Rahuki Minor canal, which is part of the Sukhur Barrage.

MARYAM IQBAL

vast aquifer exists under the Indus Plain, recharged by rain and river flows. Almost all of the Indus basin's run off has been captured through the development of large-scale irrigation schemes over the last 50 years, and the scope for further increase in water resources is limited. Unlined canals have proved to be extremely inefficient, losing large quantities of water in transmission.

A further problem is the increasing contamination of groundwater and surface-water from agricultural chemicals, and industrial and municipal wastes.

Agricultural production is threatened by land degradation. Only about 20 percent (20 million ha) of the land area of Pakistan is classified as cultivable – equal to the area already under cultivation. Much of the land is of medium to poor quality, ravaged by water and wind erosion, salinity, waterlogging, flooding and loss of organic matter. More than 96 per cent of cropland contains less than adequate organic matter. Due to the pressure on land, unsuitable areas are being used for agricultural production. Crops are not selected to match soil quality, and crop rotation is not practised properly.

Widespread and unregulated use of pesticides and fertilisers, promoted by multinationals and permitted by the government, is leading to untold long-term damage to the land and those who work on it. Women who pick cotton, for example, develop severe skin complaints from the pesticides used on the crop.

The livelihoods of pastoralists are seriously threatened, because rangelands are being over-grazed without any rehabilitation measures. Land distribution in most of Pakistan remains lopsided, with a small percentage of landlords owning a large proportion of cultivable land.

Water collecting on low-lying land. In the past, this was productive agricultural land, but water-logging has meant that crops can no longer be grown.

MARYAM IQBAL

Salinity and waterlogging

The Indus basin area of Sindh has been used for rain-fed and irrigated agriculture for thousands of years. But earlier this century, under British rule, a huge modern irrigation scheme was constructed, involving 19 barrages, 43 main canals covering more than 37,000 square miles, and more than 89,000 small water courses, to irrigate over 40 million acres of land. It is one of the largest irrigated areas in the world, and has more irrigated land than there is in the whole of Africa. Now cotton, sugar, mangoes, and guavas are grown as cash crops, both for sale within the country and for export. The scheme has alleviated poverty, but has also widened the gap between rich and poor, and the environmental cost has been enormous. The impressive growth rate in agriculture that followed large-scale irrigation is faltering

Over the years, the water-table has risen. This was a welcome result to begin with, but has led to waterlogging and salinity, because more and more water is collecting in the Indus basin area, and less and less flowing into the Arabian sea. The impact of waterlogging is determined by its combination with other factors like water quality, soil type, and precipitation/evaporation ratios. Sindh is the province worst affected by waterlogging. Within the affected area, the water table is now within 5 feet of the surface.

A major internationally-funded project – the Left Bank Outfall Drain – is now under way to try and solve the problem. Due for completion in 1992, best estimates are that it will not be fully operational until after the year 2000. A network of drainage canals is to run along the left bank of the Indus in Sindh, and a system of tube wells is to be built which will pump excess water into these canals.

Local people have little faith in mega-projects, of which there have been many, with no significant results, because they have no way of influencing the design or

Collecting water from a shallow well. The water-table is very close to the surface in this part of Sindh.

outcome. Fields are still waterlogged and land is still degrading.

In addition to widespread water-logging, 1,961,000 hectares of land in the irrigated areas is now covered by white salty crust and is uncultivable. Every year between 10 and 15 million tons of salt are added to the Indus basin. As land has become unproductive, people are being forced to migrate to other areas. The loss of income amounts to around $2.5bn. Salinity occurs when either the water-table rises to a point where evaporation leaves behind salts on the surface; or with application of water that has a high content of dissolved solids which on evaporation brings salts to the surface. The waters of the Indus have very little dissolved solids and therefore do not create salinity. But ground water, even when fresh and sweet, does have greater solid content and can in some instances be hazardous. The greatest incidence of salinity and sodicity, is in Sindh and Punjab. Sindh has about 23 per cent of its surveyed land area affected by salinity and Punjab 13 per cent.

55

Rehabilitation and regeneration

The mango trees had been slowly drowning over the years. The waterlogged soil was rotting their roots. When, in 1992, the monsoon rains came, it seemed they would never cease. The Mangla Dam reservoirs were dangerously over-full, so the sluice gates had to be opened and protective embankments along the rivers and canals breached. The waters overflowed and inundated hundreds of villages on the banks of the River Jhelum and the Indus. Pabban was one of the villages.

Pabban is a village of smallholders (1 to 10 acres) and landless peasants. Although they could see the flood coming, and could take themselves and their belongings to safety, they could not carry their mango trees with them. The floodwater stood for four weeks. 'It took us years to grow these mango trees', said an old farmer in Pabban. 'Our land is so fertile, and our mangos are some of the best in the world. But the rising water table was already starting to kill our trees. The flood has simply killed them quickly.'

The land was now so waterlogged that even the regular wheat crop could not be sown. Rose farms in the area were wiped out, houses destroyed, and belongings damaged. The villagers were in despair. And then a group of activists swung into action. In the past they had been involved in welfare work, but they now decided to focus on protecting people's livelihoods. Pabban Fruit Farmers, as they called themselves, decided to rehabilitate the orchards, to generate assets for the landless, and to gain long-term control over waterlogging and salinity.

They have replanted mango saplings as well as the more water resistant cheekoo and guava trees on 65 acres belonging to the 23 poorest families. Eleven landless peasants have together leased a block of 11 acres, which is being planted with eucalyptus supplied from the organisation's plant nursery. The eucalyptus will help to lower the water-table in the immediate area where they are planted. They have installed piezometers on the land, and even non-literate people can use this simple technology to measure the water-table level.

The saplings have been carefully tended, and are flourishing. The piezometers show the difference in the land planted with eucalyptus. A women's block forestry scheme has been set up, and the organisation is planning another land reclamation project. Rekindled hope and self-confidence is visible on the faces of the people of Pabban.

Tending the eucalyptus saplings in the women's block forestry scheme, Pabban.

MARYAM IQBAL

Vanishing forests

Pakistan's estimated forest cover of 5.2 per cent is one of the lowest in the world. Of the total area under forests 43 per cent is coniferous forests, 38 per cent scrub forests, 12 per cent is made up of mangrove forests, and the rest is irrigated plantations and riverine forests. Hill forests are the main source of timber for construction and provide large quantities of fuelwood and resin, and fodder for millions of cattle, goats, sheep and camels. Growing in the country's major watersheds, these forests contribute significantly to mitigation of floods and droughts in the plains.

The foothill forests, consisting mostly of bushes and stunted trees, provide important grazing areas and protection of watersheds and wildlife. Riverine forests along the southern part of the Indus produce high-value timber for the coal-mining and furniture industries, as well as fuelwood and charcoal. Wood provides 60 per cent of household energy and the demand for fuelwood in the country is likely to increase if the current population growth rate persists and cheap alternative fuels are not developed.

The mangroves along the coast of Sindh and Balochistan are integral to the life-cycles of many marine animals, providing important breeding sites. They also act as coastal protection barriers. The mangroves are under grave threat due to the increasing levels of sewage and industrial pollution, increased salinity in the Indus delta, and through cutting for fodder and fuel.

Forests have been used unsustainably in Pakistan and significant reduction in forest cover has occurred over the last 30 to 40 years. Much of this decrease is attributed to illegal lopping and felling, both by poor people (including Afghan refugees in NWFP and Baluchistan in the last few years, for cooking and warmth in the winter), and also by the 'timber mafia' as it is now known.

Collecting fuel-wood, Baluchistan.

DAVE TOMSON

Sungi takes on the timber mafia

After raging floods washed down villages and tore away crops in 1992, the inhabitants of Hazara district became even more aware of how deforestation had become a crucial issue for them. Sungi, a development organisation, organised public meetings in a number of villages in the area to thrash out an action plan to save their forests from ruthless cutting, and develop a strategy for community-based forest management. These meetings were attended by ordinary village people, local government officials, and representatives from the forest department.

Forests are depleted by livestock grazing, and cutting by the local people for fuel, but the major factor in the dramatic forest depletion in this area is what has been described as the 'timber mafia'. Rich and powerful, these loggers have lucrative contracts, political connections, and friends among government officials and law enforcement officers.

In one village, when Sungi tried to organise a pubic meeting on forests and people, they could not find anywhere to hold it. Although most meetings were held in the local school, threats against the school forced it to withdraw permission for the meeting to be held on its premises. Local members of Sungi were interrogated by the police and told to cancel the meeting. But they went ahead and held an open-air meeting. Some 300 people attended, including a good number of plainclothes and uniformed police.

Despite serious intimidation Sungi activists are still working in the area, continuing to organise public meetings, and helping the community to protect their forests. The meetings are always attended by a large contingent of police, busy taking notes.

The National Conservation Strategy

The government has made a serious attempt to respond to the environmental crisis and to address future needs by commissioning and publishing the National Conservation Strategy. This provides a candid review of the state of Pakistan's environment, its past and present policies and institutional mechanisms. Developed through a consultative process involving policy makers, sectoral experts and non-government organisations, the NCS has identified priority actions for immediate attention: maintaining soils in croplands; protecting watersheds; supporting forestry and plantations; restoring rangelands and improving livestock; conserving biodiversity; increasing energy efficiency; and controlling pollution.

Recommending sustainable development as the philosophy for policy-making the NCS envisages implementation through 'greater public partnership in development and management; combining environment and economics in the decision making process; and focusing on durable improvements in the quality of life.' The overriding objective of the NCS is to reverse the trend of environmental degradation and to involve local people in the effort.

NGOs in Pakistan

In both rural and urban areas in Pakistan, there is a tradition of local organisation, led either by philanthropists or community activists. These organisations have predominantly concentrated on social welfare activities, and seldom challenged social inequalities. (The organisations which address social questions would tend to act under a party political banner, or be attached to the trade union movement.) Some local 'social' organisations are taking the first steps towards an involvement in development activities, but in general, the NGO sector in Pakistan is weaker than in other countries in South Asia.

Some NGOs concentrate on advocacy and lobbying. Many direct their activities at the government and policy-making bodies, with little involvement at the grassroots. An NGO called The Network is one example, which lobbies the government on the rational use of drugs along WHO guidelines (see page 51). A more widely-based organisation is the Human Rights Commission of Pakistan, which works at many levels, from the grassroots and the streets, to parliament and the courts of justice.

In recent years, the voluntary education movement has grown dramatically. In both urban and rural areas, groups of educated, unemployed young people have got together to organise street schools. Although genuinely based in the communities they serve, most of these groups lack an analysis of poverty and poverty-focused development, and have little administrative capacity.

Two important NGOs have had a major impact on development thinking in Pakistan in both the public and NGO sectors, and provide innovative models for others to follow. The Aga Khan Rural Support Programme has pioneered an approach of building up village organisations, with separate groups for men and for women, and then launching development activities through the strengthened groups. In Karachi, the Orangi Pilot Project has been equally influential in urban development, working for the upgrading of one of Karachi's worst slum areas firstly through a sanitation scheme and following up by a range of community development activities.

In complete contrast to these large-scale NGOs are the grassroots village organisations. Run by village activists, these organisations are sometimes backed by the village elder, but may also be in opposition to the village hierarchy. Originally involved in welfare activities, such as providing school books for the poorest children, they may also be active in lobbying local authorities for electricity or water supplies, or a teacher for the village school. Now some of these groups are wanting to move towards a more developmental approach, and many have started working with their communities on environmental projects, income-generation schemes, and awareness raising.

Recently, a new kind of NGO has grown up in Pakistan, based on experience of voluntary work in disasters. Many young people have become involved in emergency work during floods or other environmental disasters, only to realise that even more needs to be done after the disaster is over, in terms of community-level rehabilitation and disaster-preparedness.

Up-date: events in Pakistan since 1996

Since this book was first published in 1996, Pakistan has experienced almost continuous turbulence, under pressure from internal tensions and external shocks. This supplement (written in March 2003) offers a brief survey of the intervening years and a description of the current political and economic situation in Pakistan.

Civilian rule, 1988–1999

In November 1996, the then President of Pakistan, Farooq Ahmed Leghari, dismissed the government of Benazir Bhutto, charging it with corruption, mismanagement of the economy, and implication in extra-judicial killings in Karachi, the provincial capital of Sindh province. An interim government took over, pending elections, which were held in February 1997 and won by the Pakistan Muslim League Party (Nawaz Group). In March 1997, with the unanimous support of the National Assembly, Prime Minister Nawaz Sharif amended the Constitution, stripping the President of the power to dismiss the government, and making his power to appoint military-service chiefs and provincial governors contingent on the

In the 1990s, leaders of NGOs campaigning against human-rights violations, such as the bonded labour of children in carpet factories, faced death threats and the prohibition of their organisations. More than 1000 were forcibly closed down in Punjab.

'advice' of the Prime Minister. Another amendment prohibited elected members from voting against party lines.

The Sharif government tried to control all major components of governance, by appointing its own supporters to the judiciary, the bureaucracy, and the ranks of political functionaries. The Prime Minister allegedly prevented the appointment of three judges approved by the then Chief Justice, Sajjad Ali Shah. With the President backing the Chief Justice, Pakistan was brought to a virtual standstill by the conflict between the executive and the judiciary. Cordial relations between the key institutions of the State were not restored until the President resigned in December 1997, and the Chief Justice was ousted by his own judges in the same month, following the storming of the Supreme Court by ruling-party loyalists. Parliament elected a new President, Rafiq Tarar, who was a close associate of the Prime Minister. The government moved to restrict press criticism and ordered the arrest and beating of prominent journalists.

The eleven-year period of civilian rule (1988–99) was a great disappointment for the people of Pakistan. The Pakistan People's Party and Muslim League (Nawaz) repeatedly accused each other of rigging elections; activists in the civil movements (for women's rights, labour rights, and human rights) were largely dissatisfied with the policies and programmes of both parties. Four general elections were held during this period; however, the infamous discriminatory laws against women were not repealed. People's confidence in democracy was undermined during this time. The government of Nawaz Sharif initiated a widespread campaign of harassment against non-government organisations: more than one thousand were closed down in Punjab alone. The Social Action Programme (1992/3–2002), costing approximately US$ 500 million, and focusing on elementary/primary education, basic health care, and the provision of rural water supplies and sanitation, proved to be a failure, owing not only to operational mismanagement by the government of Pakistan but also to foreign donors' limited understanding of the Pakistani context, as well as weak systems of collaboration and co-ordination.

The military coup – and after

On 12 October 1999, General Pervez Musharraf overthrew the civilian regime in a bloodless coup. A Proclamation of Emergency and a Provisional Constitutional Order were issued, according to which the 1973 Constitution was put in abeyance; the National Assembly, the Provincial Assemblies, and the Senate were suspended; all the State office holders, save the President of the Republic, also stood suspended, while the whole country came under the indirect rule of the Armed Forces of Pakistan. General Musharraf assumed the position of Chief Executive, ruling the country through Chief Executive's Orders. Nawaz Sharif, now the ex-Prime Minister, was exiled to Saudi Arabia. The military regime was at first welcomed by many people in Pakistan, harassed by heavy taxes and rising inflation, and hoping for economic reforms.

Musharraf appointed a National Security Council, with a mix of military/civilian appointees, a civilian Cabinet, and a National Reconstruction Bureau (NRB) to formulate structural reforms. The NRB devised a plan for the devolution of power, under which district governments have been established through elections, and political power has been devolved to the districts and sub-district levels. The system is still evolving, and financial transfer formulas are being worked out gradually. Programmes to develop the capacity of district administrations are also under way.

A National Accountability Bureau (NAB), headed by a military officer, is prosecuting those accused of wilful default on bank loans and corrupt practices; conviction may result in disqualification from political office for 21 years. The NAB Ordinance has attracted criticism for being selective in its choice of targets, and for holding the accused without charge and, in some instances, without access to legal counsel.

Military trial courts were not established, but in January 2000 the government stipulated that justices in the Supreme, High, and Shari'a Courts should swear allegiance to the Provisional Constitutional Order (PCO) and the Chief Executive. Under the PCO and its amendments, all power flows from and to the Chief Executive, and the judiciary is proscribed from issuing any order contrary to his decisions. The President, Cabinet, National Security Council, and Governors serve at his discretion. Most of the justices acquiesced, but a small minority were not invited to take the oath and were forcibly retired. In practice, Musharraf consults extensively with his civilian appointees and Corps Commanders, and in certain policy areas (such as economic reform) civilian appointees have been able to exercise considerable latitude.

In an effort to legitimise the military government, on 12 May 2000 the Supreme Court issued a judgement declaring that the army's seizure of power had become inevitable – thus validating the coup by a 'doctrine of necessity'. The judgement set a deadline for the restoration of the constitutional order through general elections to be held by 12 October 2002, three years after the military take-over.

The Khoj Network on Communication and Development works in poor communities in Lahore, organising literacy classes for women and helping them to obtain identity cards, which entitle them to vote in local and national elections.

LIZ CLAYTON/OXFAM

The task of devolving power was assigned to the National Reconstruction Bureau, which developed a system of local government through research and nation-wide consultations. In 2001, local elections were held for the third time in Pakistan's history. For the first time ever, legal provisions were made for a proportion (33 per cent) of the seats in local elections to be reserved for women.

On 20 June 2001, General Musharraf became President of Pakistan and took oath. In April 2002, a controversial referendum extended the duration of his presidential term for another five years. Elections were held on 10 October 2002, but no political party won a majority of the votes cast. However, the Pakistan Muslim League has formed a government, in coalition with Muttahida Mahaz-e-Amal – United Action Front (MMA), a coalition of religious parties, with Mr Jamali as Prime Minister. For the past two decades, religious organisations have become more and more organised and have been actively taking part in the political arena, with limited success so far. Now MMA has won a clear majority in North West Frontier Province, and a majority sufficient to form the government in Baluchistan Province. At the national level, MMA has won nearly 50 seats.

This situation places responsibility for law and order on the shoulders of the religious parties and challenges them to fulfil their promises to create a just and fair Pakistan. Although there are fears that laws discriminating against women may be promoted by MMA, there has so far been no such indication. Ironically, during the first session of the national assembly in October 2002, neither the representative from the People's Party nor the representative of Pakistan Muslim League (Quaid-e-Azam Group) mentioned women in his introductory speech; the first speaker who mentioned women's rights was Qazi Hussain Ahmed, representing the right-wing coalition of religious parties.

In the National Assembly, there are 72 women out of a total of 332 members; 60 of them occupy reserved seats, while 12 were selected in open contests. Cynics have observed that most of them are from the long-established so-called 'political' families and may not all be sensitive to matters of gender-fair governance.

President Musharraf's decision to side with the USA and support its 'war on terrorism' has been met in Pakistan with mixed feelings. Although people understand that Pakistan was given no choice in the matter, the general feeling is that the government should have imposed some conditions before agreeing to becoming the frontline State in the service of US political interests in the region.

External relations
Pakistan and India
Relations between Pakistan and India have always been strained, for many reasons, dating back to the violence that attended the partition of India in 1947. Pakistan owes its existence to the 'two-nation theory', which held that Hindus and Muslims had distinct identities and could not co-exist within one State. Behind this argument was a real fear that, once the British had left, the Hindus would take revenge on Muslims for their thousand-year rule, not all of it benevolent. But the process of partition was too hasty, and systems of governance and infrastructure collapsed as hundreds of thousands of people began migrating from both India and Pakistan, and communal clashes occurred all over the country. Thousands of people, members of every ethnic and religious group, lost their lives and their livelihoods in the aftermath.

Pakistan and India have been at war four times since the partition in 1947, and their dispute over the status of Kashmir remains unresolved. As both States possess nuclear weapons, there is a grave danger that any conflict between them might escalate into a war of mass destruction, with widespread and unforeseen consequences. At the time of partition, the princely state of Kashmir, although ruled by a Hindu Maharajah, had an overwhelmingly Muslim population. When the Maharajah hesitated in acceding either to Pakistan or to India in 1947, some of his Muslim subjects, aided by tribesmen from Pakistan, revolted in favour of joining Pakistan. In exchange for military assistance in containing the revolt, the Kashmiri ruler offered his allegiance to India. Indian troops occupied the eastern portion of Kashmir, including its capital, Srinagar, while the western part came under Pakistani control.

In 1949, the United Nations arranged a ceasefire along a line dividing Kashmir, but leaving the northern end of the line undemarcated and the Vale of Kashmir (home to the majority of the population) under Indian control. Pakistan agreed to India's call for a UN-supervised plebiscite to determine the future of the State, but the plebiscite never took place because India repeatedly postponed it.

In September 1965 a full-scale war broke out, ending three weeks later in response to mediation by the UN and interested countries. Indian and Pakistani representatives met in Tashkent, in the former USSR, and agreed to attempt a peaceful settlement of the conflict over Kashmir and their other differences. But in 1971 another conflict began, this time lasting almost a year, with four weeks of full-blown war, fought mainly in East Pakistan and resulting in the fall of Dhaka on 16 December 1971. President Zulfiqar Ali Bhutto and Indian Prime Minister Indira Gandhi agreed to the establishment of a line of control in Kashmir, and endorsed the principle of settling bilateral disputes through peaceful means. In 1974, Pakistan and India agreed to resume postal and telecommunications links, and to enact measures to facilitate travel. Trade and diplomatic relations were restored in 1976 after a break of five years.

India's nuclear test in 1974 generated great uncertainty in Pakistan and is generally acknowledged to have been the impetus for Pakistan's nuclear weapons development programme. In recent years, the Indo-Pakistani relationship has fluctuated between rapprochement and conflict. Prime Minister Nawaz Sharif moved to resume official dialogue with India in 1997. A number of meetings took place, with little progress towards peace in the region, although generally the atmosphere improved.

Under a pro-Hindu fundamentalist government, India exploded a nuclear device in 1998. The government of Nawaz Sharif promptly responded by exploding its own device in Chaghi district, Baluchistan, in defiance of pacifists in Pakistan and pressure from international community, but to the jubilation of common people in Pakistan.

Indian Prime Minister Vajpayee travelled to Lahore for a summit meeting with Sharif in February 1999, but hopes of a positive breakthrough were dashed a few weeks later, when infiltrators from Pakistan occupied positions on the Indian side of the Line of Control in the remote, mountainous area of Kashmir near Kargil. They cut Indian supply lines to forces stationed on Siachen Glacier. By early summer, serious fighting had flared in the Kargil sector. The conflict ended after a meeting between Prime Minister Sharif and US President Clinton in July 1999. Relations between India and Pakistan have thereafter been particularly strained, especially since the military coup in Islamabad in October 1999.

After the terrorist attacks on New York and Washington in September 2001, India quickly offered to co-operate with the US government in fighting terrorism and routing Osama bin Laden. India saw it as an opportunity to strengthen relations with the USA and hoped that the US 'war on terrorism' would be extended to target the Kashmiri militants. However, the US government chose to make Pakistan its frontline State. Pakistan now feels that it has an opportunity to pursue a proactive policy on Kashmir, one that combines deft and imaginative diplomacy with overt efforts to alter the *status quo*. Certainly, the United States is now more receptive to Pakistan's argument that an inextricable link exists between a settlement of the problem of Kashmir and the quest for a durable peace between South Asia's two nuclear-armed adversarial neighbours. But with India and Pakistan each aspiring to gain total control over Kashmir, and the people living in the Pakistan-controlled area (known as 'Azad Jammu and Kashmir') aspiring

Quetta, Baluchistan, 2001: trucks loaded with food for refugees from drought-ridden Afghanistan

This stone cairn in Baluchistan marks the official border between Pakistan and Afghanistan.

to establish an independent state of their own, a peaceful solution seems as far off as ever.

In global terms, Kashmir, like Palestine, is a major flashpoint, but there is a significant difference between the two cases: in South Asia, a million men under arms are facing each other in an eyeball-to-eyeball confrontation which could spin out of control and lead to the deployment of nuclear weapons.

Pakistan and Afghanistan

According to the website of the Pakistani Ministry of Foreign Affairs, 'Pakistan supports a united, stable and prosperous Afghanistan. Pakistan's primary objective in Afghanistan is the restoration of durable peace and it supports any formula that is acceptable to Afghan parties. Pakistan has always condemned external interference in the internal affairs of Afghanistan.'

After the Soviets invaded Afghanistan in 1979, the Pakistani government played a vital role in supporting the Afghan resistance movement and in hosting and assisting Afghan refugees. In February 1989, the Soviets withdrew from Afghanistan, but Pakistan continued to provide support for displaced Afghans, with co-operation from the world community, multilateral organisations, and NGOs. By 1999, more than 1.2 million registered Afghan refugees

remained in Pakistan, as fighting between rival factions in their home country continued. Pakistan formally recognised the Taliban as the government in Afghanistan and gave them assistance. The government of Pakistan has periodically offered to try to bring Afghanistan's warring factions to the negotiating table.

Pakistan claims that it has suffered more than any other country from the continuation of the conflict in Afghanistan. The government website states: 'For us, vital security interests are linked to stability on our western and northern borders. We therefore seek peace, stability and national reconciliation in Afghanistan. This will open new opportunities in our economic and commercial relations with the Central Asian States.' General Musharraf was one of the first visitors to Afghanistan after the Taliban govern-ment fell. His purpose was to establish good relations with the new regime, and reconfirm Pakistan's solidarity with Afghan people. He handed a cheque for US$10 million to Chairman Karzai of Afghanistan, as part of a $100 million package of aid, offered without conditions for the reconstruction of Afghanistan. Pakistan also provided airplanes for Afghan pilgrims travelling to Saudi Arabia. These measures have helped to create a conducive environ-ment for Pakistani businesses to invest in the reconstruction of Afghanistan, which should eventually pay financial dividends to Pakistani traders.

In the field of economic co-operation, Karzai and Musharraf took a major decision: to form a Joint Ministerial Commission (JMC) to promote bilateral economic and trade links. The JMC would also help to co-ordinate reconstruction efforts in Afghanistan. The two governments have discussed the recommencement of air flights between the two countries, and the use of Pakistan's seaport for the transportation of the equipment and material to be used in the reconstruction of landlocked Afghanistan.

Drought in Afghanistan has increased the volume of food imports from Pakistan, but re-exports of consumer goods to Pakistan are much lower, because of tight border controls and reduced consumer demand in Pakistan. Overall, the trade from Pakistan has helped Afghanistan to generate incomes, provide employment, and increase supplies of basic goods, including food in the current drought.

According to the UN High Commissioner for Refugees, approximately 1.5 million Afghan refugees had returned home by August 2002, and an estimated 2 million still remained in Pakistan, given the continuing instability of political, economic, and security conditions in Afghanistan.

Pakistan and the USA

The United States and Pakistan established diplomatic relations in 1947. The USA agreed to provide economic and military assistance to Pakistan, but military aid was suspended during the 1965 Pakistan–India war. This gave rise to a widespread feeling of betrayal in Pakistan. Financial support from the USA has been proffered, withdrawn, and resumed several times, often without notice, and always in response to the strategic concerns of the superpower. Although the people of

Pakistan respect US knowledge and technical expertise, there is a growing suspicion that the US government will only exploit Pakistan, use it for its own ends, and abandon it eventually.

Since 11 September 2001, anti-American feelings have run high in Pakistan. The US bombing of Afghanistan did not have grassroots support, and civilian deaths in Afghanistan have not made the USA any more popular in Pakistan. More recently, the US attack on Iraq brought hundreds of thousands of Pakistani people out in peaceful protests on the streets, demanding an immediate end to the war and a strong government stance on the issue. The Pakistan government condemned the conflict, but refrained from overt criticism of the USA. However, a prolonged war would almost certainly increase anti-American sentiments at the popular level.

The economy

Pakistan has a great potential for economic growth, possessing as it does significant natural resources and entrepreneurial skills. However, that potential has not been realised for the benefit of the mass of the population, for many reasons: the inequitable distribution of income, a less than effective tax-collection system, an unmet need for land reforms, and fiscal mismanagement which has resulted in a large foreign debt. Debt servicing and the defence budget impose a heavy burden on the economy. Although Pakistan averaged an impressive growth rate of 6 per cent per year during the 1980s and early 1990s, the economy is vulnerable to internal tensions and external shocks. For instance, in 1992–93, floods and political instability reduced economic growth, and the financial crisis in Asia hit major markets for Pakistani textile exports. Average real GDP growth from 1992 to 1998 dipped to 4.1 per cent.

Pakistan has been pursuing market-based economic reforms since the 1980s. In 1988 the government launched a structural adjustment programme with the assistance of the International Monetary Fund. A number of initiatives were undertaken: barriers to foreign trade and investment were removed; there were attempts to reform the financial system; foreign-exchange controls were eased; several State-owned enterprises were privatised. Even today, Pakistan continues to struggle with these reforms, but with mixed success. The rupee was continually devalued until very recently, when US involvement in Afghanistan strengthened the value of Pakistan's currency.

Agriculture

Arable land and water are Pakistan's principal natural resources, although water shortages have begun to occur in the past decade. Approximately 25 per cent of Pakistan's total land area is under cultivation and is watered by one of the largest artificial irrigation systems in the world. Agriculture accounts for about 24 per cent of GDP and employs about 50 per cent of the labour force. The most important crops are wheat, sugar-cane, cotton, and rice, which together account for more than 75 per cent of the value of total crop output. The government assists farmers by supporting prices and providing easy credit. Agricultural initiatives, including increased production of wheat and oilseed, play a central role in the new government's economic reform package.

Energy

Pakistan has considerable reserves of natural gas, oil, and coal, and large hydro-electric potential. However, the exploitation of energy resources has been frustrated by a shortage of capital and by political constraints. Domestic petroleum production meets only about half the country's needs for oil; the rest has to be imported. The current government has announced that privatisation of these resources is a priority, and attempts are being made to use indigenous gas instead of imported oil, thus saving precious reserves of foreign currency.

SARAH ERRINGTON/OXFAM

Women watering livestock: farming employs about 50 per cent of the labour force in Pakistan.

Industry

Pakistan's manufacturing sector accounts for about 26 per cent of GDP. Cotton textile production and clothing manufacture are Pakistan's largest industries, accounting for about 64 per cent of total exports. Other major industries include the production of cement, fertiliser, edible oil, sugar, steel, tobacco, chemicals, and machinery, and also food processing. The government has been trying to privatise many State-controlled industrial units. Pakistan provides adequate formal legal protections for foreign investment, but, due to sectarian and ethnic violence and a poorly educated workforce, foreign investment is limited.

ANNIE BUNGEROTH/OXFAM

Allahwadin, a street boy in Quetta, with his pet partridge, which he keeps in a cage at the garbage depot where he sells scrap metal. Allahwaddin is learning to read at an Oxfam-funded drop-in centre for street boys.

Poverty

Almost one third of the people of Pakistan, mainly in rural areas, live below the official poverty line, in the sense that they regularly go hungry. Per capita government expenditure on health care is currently only US$ 2 a year – well below regional and international comparators. Access to education and other services is limited, especially in the countryside, and women and girls are at a particular disadvantage.

With a per capita GDP of about US$ 1928, the World Bank considers Pakistan a low-income country. No more than 45 per cent of adults are literate, and life expectancy is about 61 years. The population, currently about 148 million, is growing at the rate of 2.1 per cent per annum, very close to the GDP growth rate. Inadequate social services and the high rate of population growth help to perpetuate poverty and the unequal distribution of wealth.

In the last three years, the government of Pakistan has implemented wide-ranging structural reforms to stimulate economic growth. An interim Poverty Reduction Strategy Paper has been developed; it highlights the needs of the poor in many sectors, including education, health care, and water supply. The devolution of political power, if successful, has the potential to improve the coverage and quality of social-service delivery for the poor, as well as encouraging their involvement in monitoring and managing the facilities. The government has also undertaken two major initiatives – Khushal Pakistan (a comprehensive poverty intervention) and Khushali Bank (a micro-credit bank) – as nationwide efforts to address poverty and vulnerability.

Supplementary text written by Bilquis Tahira, March 2003.

Facts and figures

MARYAM IQBAL/OXFAM

Area	770,880 sq km
Population	148,721,000 (2002)
Population growth rate	2.1% (2001)
Urban population	37%
Major cities	Karachi, 11,800,000; Lahore 5,470,000; Islamabad 1,018,000
Languages	Punjabi, Pushto, Sindhi, Saraiki, Urdu, Balochi, Hindko, Brohi
Religious affiliations	Muslim 97%, Christian 1.5%, Hindu 1.5%
Adult literacy	43% (male 58%; female 28%)
Life expectancy	61 years
Infant mortality	85 (per 1000 live births)
Health care	One doctor per 1754 persons; one hospital bed for 1555 persons
Communications	22 telephone lines per 1000 people
Principal exports	Garments, cotton, rice, leather and leather goods, fresh fish, textiles, sports goods
Principal imports	Machinery, petroleum, petroleum products, chemicals, transportation equipment, edible oils, grains, pulses, flour
Main trading partners	Exports: USA, UK, UAE, Hong Kong, Germany
	Imports: Kuwait, UAE, Saudi Arabia, USA, Japan
Foreign debt	$32 billion
Form of government	Parliamentary, federal Islamic republic, with two legislative houses; Senate 87 members; National Assembly members 357
Human Development Index	138 (out of 173) (2002)

(All figures relate to the year 2000 unless otherwise specified. Sources: United Nations and The World Bank, quoted in *The World Guide 2003/2004.*)

Entrance to a shrine, Multan

Further reading

M. Rafique Afzal *Pakistan: History and Politics* 1947-1971 (Oxford: Oxford University Press, 2002)

Shakil Akhtar *Media, Religion, and Politics in Pakistan* (Oxford: Oxford University Press, 2000)

Selig Harrison et al. (eds.) *India and Pakistan: The First Fifty Years* (Cambridge: Cambridge University Press, 1998)

Christophe Jaffrelot (ed.) *Pakistan: Nationalism without a Nation?* (London: Zed Books, 2002)

Christophe Jaffrelot (ed.) *A History of Pakistan and its Origins* (London: Anthem Press, 2002)

Owen Bennett Jones *Pakistan: The Eye of the Storm* (New Haven, Connecticut: Yale University Press, 2002)

Ahmed Rashid *Militant Islam, Oil and Fundamentalism in Central Asia* (New Haven, Connecticut:Yale University Press, 2001)

Victoria Schofield *Kashmir in Conflict: India, Pakistan, and the Unfinished War* (London: I.B. Tauris, 2000)

Ian Talbot *Pakistan: A Modern History* (Basingstoke: Palgrave Macmillan, 1999)

Mary Anne Weaver *Pakistan: In the Shadow of Jihad and Afghanistan* (New York: Farrar, Straus & Giroux, 2002)

Lawrence Ziring *Pakistan in the Twentieth Century: A Political History* (Oxford: Oxford University Press, 1998)

SARAH ERRINGTON/OXFAM

Oxfam in Pakistan

Oxfam GB has funded relief and development work in Pakistan since 1973. Its first office was opened in 1989, to administer a programme which delivered welfare services to communities in need. Today Oxfam has four offices in Pakistan, and its staff work mainly through partnerships with local grassroots groups, intermediary NGOs, and campaigning organisations, strengthening them to undertake sustainable development work of their own. Poor communities are empowered to claim their basic human rights in a wide range of contexts: education, health care, natural-resource management, disasters and emergencies, and women's rights.

In the field of education, Oxfam in Pakistan supports programmes which address the particular needs of girls and women, who are at a severe disadvantage, especially in rural areas, where boys are three times more likely than girls to complete their primary education, and literacy rates for women are in some places as low as 9 per cent. Oxfam's partner, Khoj, has developed innovative teaching methods which accelerate learning and are relevant to women's lives. Its students acquire the self-confidence to play a fuller part in society: for example, Najma, who was illiterate five years ago, had the courage to run for local council elections in 2002. Oxfam also funds the development of educational resources which challenge conventional assumptions about gender roles, and supports partners' efforts to lobby the government to improve school-enrolment rates for girls and improve the quality of education.

Oxfam is committed to the campaign to end violence against women.

It supports awareness-raising projects such as street theatre, advertisements in cinemas, and poster competitions; community workshops in districts where 'honour killings' of women by male relatives are most prevalent have also been supported. Oxfam funds legal aid and para-legal training programmes, with some notable successes: in a village near Islamabad, for example, young girls educated through the para-legal programme have been able to negotiate better marriage contracts, which give them more rights and protection under the laws.

In the field of health care, Oxfam works to improve the supply of affordable medicines to poor people, and especially to women and children. Its partner on this issue is forming a network to lobby the government to challenge policies of the World Trade Organisation which disadvantage developing countries like Pakistan.

In rural areas, farmers' groups are supported in their efforts to manage local natural resources in a sustainable manner, with a particular emphasis on

The Khoj Network on Communication and Development, supported by Oxfam, teaches literacy and computer skills to girls and women in poor communities of Lahore.

ANNIE BUNGEROTH/OXFAM

cleaning up water-sources and reclaiming degraded land. In response to the natural disasters that regularly afflict Pakistan, Oxfam is working with government institutions and other emergency-relief organisations to develop programmes to deal with droughts and cyclones. Communities suffering from years of drought in Baluchistan have been supported by food-distribution and asset-building programmes which are gradually being converted into rehabilitation and livelihoods-support work.

In 2002, Oxfam set up water-supply and hygiene-promotion systems in four camps, serving more than fifty thousand refugees from the crisis in Afghanistan. Oxfam has also supported displaced communities along the line of control in Kashmir, bringing water nearer to their homes, in order to avoid the landmines laid in nearby rivers. In the same year, Oxfam was the first NGO to arrive with relief supplies after an earthquake struck in the north of Pakistan; in harsh winter conditions, staff collaborated with the government and other agencies to distribute tents and food. Oxfam is also working with the Punjab provincial government to develop a policy on disasters and relief management.

Oxfam's long-term objective in Pakistan is to develop the capacity of intermediary civil-society organisations: helping them to acquire skills and improve their internal systems and their external links, in order to work for justice and equality at all levels of society.